November 28, 1991

Dear Mick, Cindy, Tanya and Kyle,

We have truly enjoyed knowing you, and hope your "new life" in San Diego will be everything you hope for.

We wish for you the best, and hope your memories of Tampa (Lutz!) will all be good ones!

Let's stay in touch.

Love,

Glady and Valerie

T·A·M·P·A

A PICTORIAL HISTORY

E.A.Clarke&Co
Clothing & Furnishing Goods

T·A·M·P·A

A PICTORIAL HISTORY

by Hampton Dunn

Design by
Paula Hennigan Phillips

The Donning Company/Publishers
Norfolk/Virginia Beach

To
"EVAN FROM HEAVEN"
My Precocious Grandson
EVAN CLARK OLDROYD
Louisville, Colorado

Library of Congress Cataloging in Publication Data

Dunn, Hampton.
Tampa: a pictorial history.

Bibliography: p.
Includes index.
1. Tampa (Fla.)—History—Pictorial works. 2. Tampa (Fla.)—Description—Views. I. Title
F319.T2D84 1985 975.9'65 85-4450
ISBN 0-89865-408-4 (a special edition)
ISBN 0-89865-409-2 (pbk.)

Printed in the United States of America

Contents

Foreword
by James A. Clendinen 7

Preface 8

Chapter I
Tampa Before 1900 11

Chapter II
1900 through 1919 43

Chapter III
1920 through 1929 69

Chapter IV
1930 through 1939 99

Chapter V
1940 through 1949 135

Chapter VI
1950 to Today 179

Bibliography 220

Index 221

About the Author 224

James A. Clendenin is Chairman of the Editorial Board Tampa Tribune, Tampa Times. *Photograph courtesy of the* Tampa Tribune

Foreword

Hampton Dunn and I arrived in Tampa the same year, he as a university student, I as a reporter for the *Tampa Tribune*. 1935. What a year! It was, in its way, as much a watershed as that year a half century earlier when the coming of Henry B. Plant's railroad transformed a shrinking village into a boom town.

In 1935 Tampa was as corrupt a city as could be found in the United States. Gambling joints and houses of prostitution ran wide open; underworld characters were in partnership with politicians; elections were so brazenly stolen that the whole state knew one of its United States senators owed his seat to Tampa's hot votes.

The turning point came in the municipal election of 1935, a struggle for power between the city hall and courthouse gangs, each of which recruited hundreds of armed hoodlums to police the polls. The threat of bloodshed was so grave that the governor sent in the National Guard to preserve order. And all this in the midst of a hurricane!

Even calloused consciences were pricked by the disgraceful state to which Tampa had fallen. Civic organizations, urged on by the newspapers, began a cleanup campaign; step by painful step over a period of years, the reformers forced the conversion of Sin City to a self-respecting and respected community.

Hampton Dunn, as a reporter for the *Tampa Daily Times* and later its managing editor, was both a recorder of this history and a participant in it. His interest in current events broadened into a lively curiosity about the historical forces of change. He has become a widely known writer and lecturer on Florida and is the author of histories of Tampa and four other Florida cities, among other publications. For ten years he wrote a column on Florida points of historical interest for *The Tribune's* Sunday magazine—and all this in addition to his full-time position as senior vice president of the Peninsula Motor Club (AAA) and editor of its 550,000-circulation publication, *Florida Explorer*.

Three governors have recognized Dunn's work by appointing him to historic preservation boards, and the Florida Historical Society has presented him its top award. Also, the American Association for State and Local History, the Tampa Historical Society, and numerous other groups have honored him.

In his book *Yesterday's Tampa* (now in its sixth printing), Dunn portrayed the history of the city from its beginnings as an Indian village and U.S. Army fort through the boom-and-bust of the twenties and the Depression of the thirties.

In this new volume Dunn revisits the city with which he has had a love affair for over half a century, reporting in words and with pictures the story of Tampa from its wilderness beginnings to its present day renaissance, a born again community bursting with activity and growth here in the 1980s. Dunn reviews the formative years of the city and picks up the Tampa story at the time he himself was able to begin observing it—that terrible but redemptive year, 1935. It is a city and a history well worth knowing. And Hampton Dunn knows it very well.

JAMES A. CLENDINEN
Chairman of the Editorial Board
Tampa Tribune

Preface

The more extensive
a man's knowledge
of what has
been done, the
greater will be his power of knowing what to do.
—Benjamin Disraeli

This year, 1985, Tampa is undergoing a metamorphosis, which is defined as "a transformation, as by magic."

The entire downtown, it seems, is being skinned, and it appears we're starting all over again. For many decades, the thirteen-story First National Bank building was our tallest structure. Now we have numerous glass houses, skyscrapers thirty-five to forty stories high changing the skyline which had been static since the Florida real estate boom of the 1920s.

In the course of this transformation, some of our beloved landmarks of yesteryear have been wiped out—the old Hillsborough County Courthouse, the Tampa Terrace Hotel, the Thomas Jefferson Hotel, Phillips Field stadium, Peter O. Knight Airport administration building, most of our Victorian mansions, and others.

But around town, other landmarks have emerged: the splendid Tampa stadium, home of our Tampa Bay Bucs, our Tampa Bay Bandits, and our Tampa Bay Rowdies; our Taj Mahal, Tampa International Airport; modern expressways criss-crossing the city; condominiums on Bayshore Boulevard; the University of South Florida; Busch Gardens; new residential areas; and shopping centers everywhere.

An endless list of "progress."

In the midst of it all, we never want to forget our colorful past. We want to preserve the familiar scenes of the past; we want to remember the people who brought Tampa this far, our pioneers and our leaders through the years. We want to keep the home-town flavor which has endeared the city to generation after generation.

What better way to present a permanent record of the way we were than through a complete pictorial history with hundreds of historical photographs?

In this volume we bring you nostalgia in wholesale lots. We jog your memories and we stir tears with those scenes of the past—many of happy times, many of sorrowful times. Obviously, it is impossible to bring a definitive history in a volume this size. We do bring you many of the highlights of the past, and we hope to stimulate history buffs, Tampaphiles, and others to reflect on their own memories to recall the sometimes drab, sometimes exciting, past.

Although there is some narrative, we rely almost exclusively on photographs to do this. Ivan Sergeyvich Turgeniev (1818-1883) once said, "A picture may instantly present what a book could set forth only in a hundred pages." A Chinese proverb claims one picture is worth more than 10,000 words, while Mark Sullivan declares, "A picture can tell more than a page of text." With all this in mind, we chose this format.

The author is fortunate to have accumulated one of the largest—if not the largest—collection of photos of Tampa. This includes the bulk of the Burgert Brothers pictures, which we obtained through Henry Cox, and the bulk of the Robertson and Fresh photos and negatives. Our own tremendous post card collection offers many dandies of historic sites and scenes, dating back before the turn of the century. Added to these are hundreds, yea thousands, of other pictures that have come to us from various sources. We are especially grateful for the contributions from fellow citizens and other history buffs who have helped build up the file.

Incidentally, we have made arrangements for the permanent safekeeping of this vast collection of Floridiana in the Special Collections Department of the University of South Florida Library where it will remain for the use of future historians and scholars researching Florida's past.

It goes without saying that many persons have contributed to the publication of this volume. At the risk of omitting some, I would like to mention a few who have pitched in and helped.

It was an honor to have our long-time friend and erstwhile competitor in the news-gathering business in Tampa—Jimmy Clendinen, now Chairman of the Editorial Board of the *Tampa Tribune*—write the interesting Foreword. His facile pen and diligent researching have provided information and inspired leadership for this community for nearly fifty years.

Also, thanks to Dr. Edgar W. Hirshberg, professor of English at the University of South Florida, to Fred E. Orr and to Michele Dickey of the Donning Company, Publishers, for editing the manuscript.

Other individuals and organizations who have contributed one way or another in putting this book together include: Sol Fleischman, my buddy in the old WDAE-The *Tampa Daily Times* days and former sportscaster for WTVT-TV; Johnny Upson, local swimming coach; Dr. James M. Ingram, medical historian; Joseph Hipp, head of special collections of the Tampa/Hillsborough County Public Library; Jay B. Dobkin, director of the special collection section, University of South Florida Library; the Reverend Earl Hartman, chairman of the Billy Graham Florida-West Coast Crusade; Mrs. Yetive Olson; Bobby Smith, Southern Photo and News; Al Hackett, Florida Division of Tourism; Jean Morris, Florida State Photographic Archives, Florida State Museum, Tallahassee; Dorothy Sappington, Elkhart, Indiana; Tony Pizzo, Tampa and Ybor City historian; the late Dale E. Friend, University of Tampa; Nancy McWilliams, Tampa News Bureau; Bob Best, Tampa Bay Buccaneers; Lori Hartsock; the late Sara Keller Hobbs; Elizabeth Carnes; Adalaide Bloch Morris; Reggie McAteer; Mrs. Temprice Ledbetter; Sophia E. Earle; Jimmy Lawhon; Vince ("Cowboy") Meloy; Mrs. Thomas Beusse; Dr. Gary Mormino—and a host of others. Thanks!

This is my book about my Tampa. Hope you enjoy it!

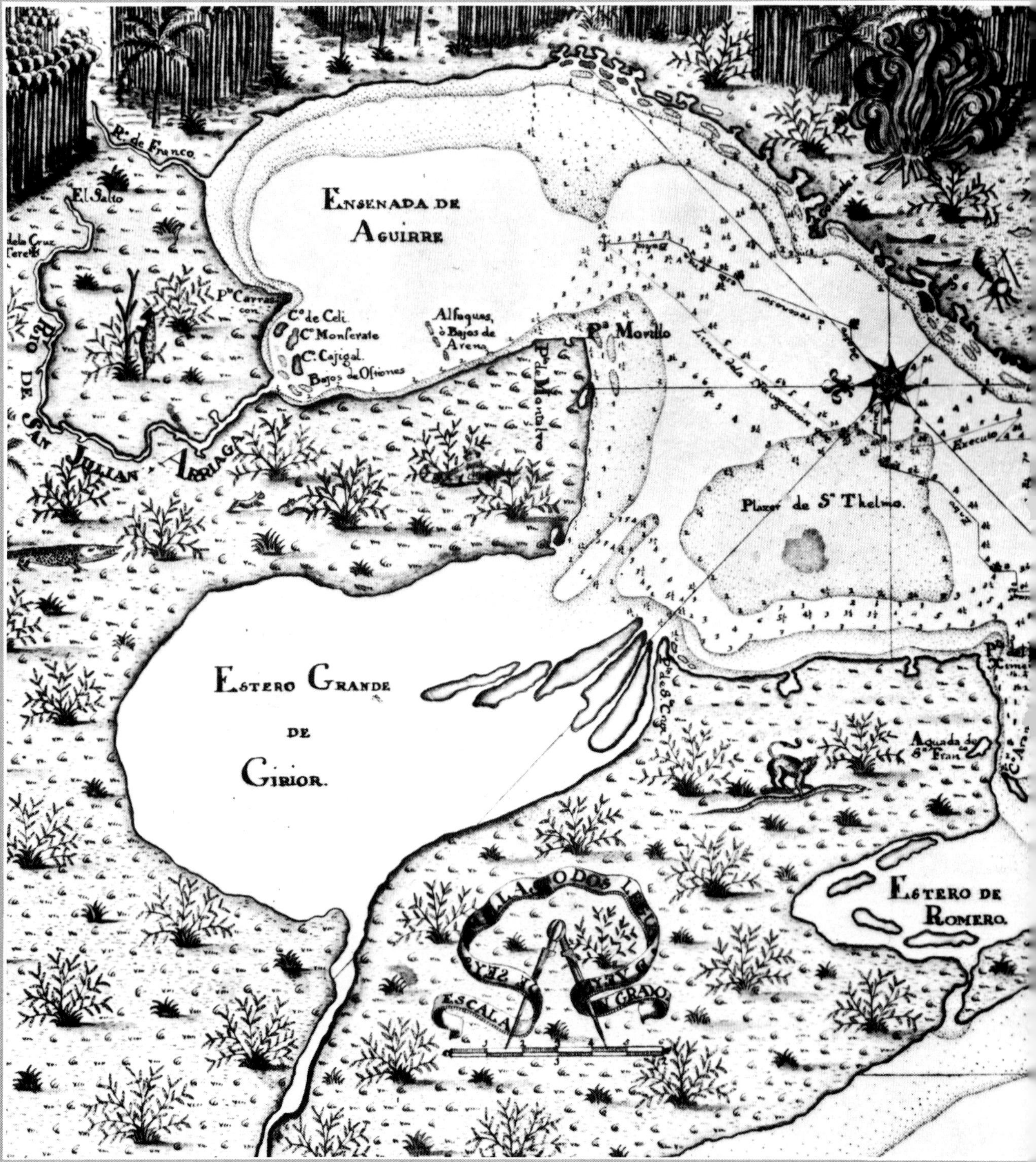

Ensenada de Aguirre
Rº de Franco
El Salto
Rio de San Julian Arriaga
Co de Celi
Co Monserrate
Co Cajigal
Bajos de Ostiones
Alfaguas, ó Bajos de Arena
Pa Morillo
Plazer de St Thelmo
Estero Grande de Girior
Estero de Romero
Escala

Chapter 1

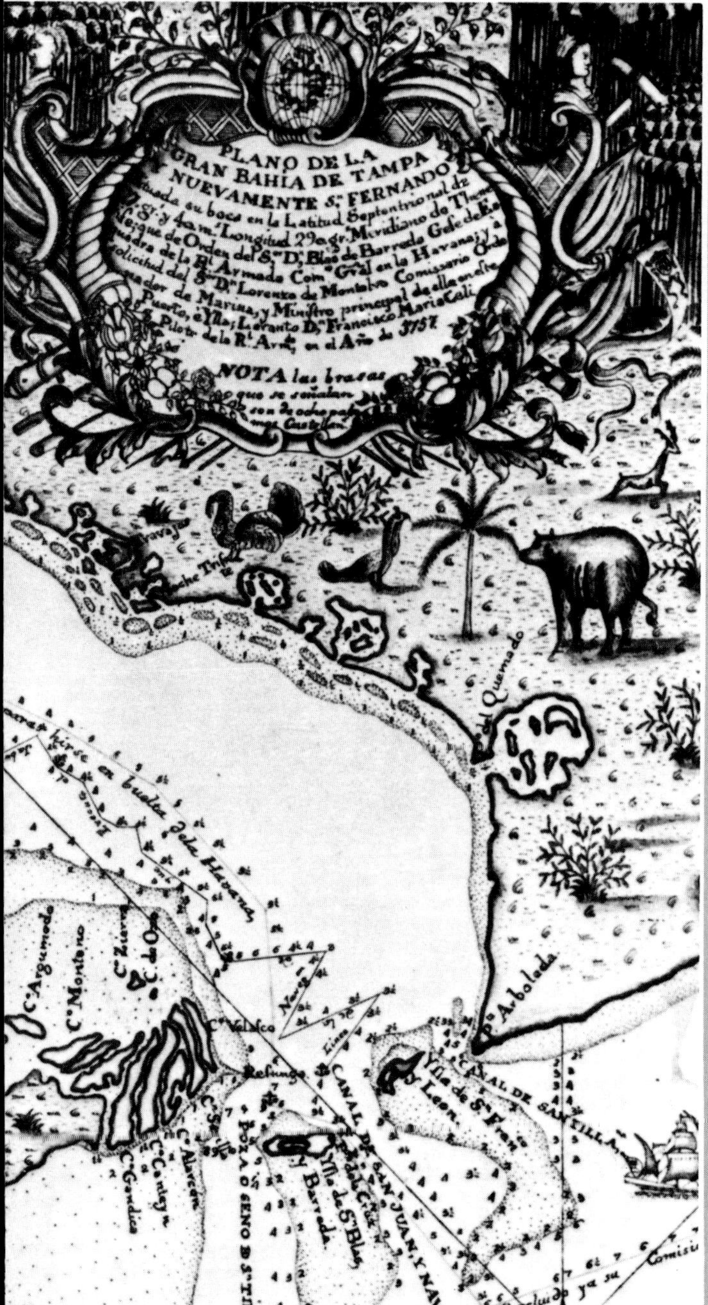

Tampa Before 1900

The Tampa Bay region properly might be called the Cradle of North America. For it was here on Florida's sparkling Gulf coast that most of the Spanish conquistadores set foot on this continent and the white man began civilizing this part of the world. Yes, there were Ponce de Leon (1521), Panfilo de Narvaez (1528), Hernando de Soto (1539), Tristan de Luna (1559), and Pedro Menendez (1565). All of this action was taking place on Florida shores long before that crowd came over on the *Mayflower* and got all the publicity!

And it was Cabeza De Vaca, official chronicler of the ill-fated de Narvaez expedition, who first labeled Tampa as "the best port in the world."

The coming of the white man spelled the beginning of the end of control of these parts by the Indians. The Calusans and Timucuans had romped and played and fished and hunted this peninsula for centuries before.

But first there had to be a war to force removal of the Indians to reservations out West. Thus, in 1824, the U.S. Army established Fort Brooke at the mouth of the Hillsborough River, with Colonel George M. Brooke commanding. A village sprang up around this base, the beginning of Tampa.

The community was involved in another war a few decades later. Tampa and Florida fought with the Confederacy in the Civil War and there were some skirmishes in the area.

Tampa took a turn for greatness with the coming of the railroad in 1884, the move here of the cigar industry in 1886, and the opening of Henry B. Plant's elegant Tampa Bay Hotel in 1891. In 1898 the city became the port of embarkation for U.S. soldiers going to Cuba to fight the Spanish-American War.

At the turn of the century, the war was over and Tampans had begun a return to normal living. There was a population explosion underway: Between 1890 and 1910. Tampa's growth was the greatest of any city in its class in the U.S.—596% increase!

"Since being a city, the growth has been nothing short of marvelous," chortled the Tampa Board of Trade.

(overleaf)
The body of water known today as Tampa Bay has a long and colorful history. The first discovery of the bay by the Spanish explorers probably occurred around 1513. It was not until 1757 that the Spanish Royal Fleet sent an expedition to explore and chart the area. The chart from this survey by Don Francisco Maria Celi is a beautifully executed and detailed document of priceless value to historians. The chart's actual whereabouts became shrouded in ambiguity over the intervening years until Tony Pizzo, well-known Tampa amateur historian, and Dr. Charles Arnade, University of South Florida professor, found it hanging in the archives of the Spanish Naval Museum in Madrid. Photograph courtesy of Tony Pizzo

Spanish explorer Panfilo de Narvaez passed through Tampa in April 1528 on his ill-fated journey into the New World. For years the bridge over the bay at Twenty-Second Street was named in his honor. When a new bridge was erected in the 1970s it acquired a new name. In this photo, author Hampton Dunn rescues the corner-stone plaque from the DeNarvaez bridge. Photograph by Tony Pizzo

When white men invaded Florida in the sixteenth century, they came upon Indian villages spotted around the peninsula. The Calusans and the Timucuans both settled in the Tampa area. The hardy breed of red men fortified their community of thatched huts, as this drawing by LeMoyne of a Timucuan settlement illustrates. Photograph of drawing by LeMoyne, from the author's collection

A pre-Columbian stone head carved by an unknown native Indian, date unknown, was found near the Columbus Drive Bridge on the Hillsborough River by Santo Rondanzo in 1968. Photograph courtesy of Kenneth W. Mulder

The Spanish conquistadores passed this way early in the sixteenth century. And here, modern-day WTVT reporter Bob Fellows announces the finding of a stone cross carved in flint head coral stone found on the east side of the Hillsborough River near the Fortieth Street Bridge in 1977 by Don Gray. It well could be a relic of Hernando DeSoto and his party who camped here in their 1539 sweep of the area. Photograph courtesy of Kenneth W. Mulder

Unidentified Seminole Indians on a visit to Tampa, probably in the 1920s. Photograph by Burgert Brothers, from the author's collection

Stern-looking Billy Bowlegs, Indian leader during the Third Seminole War (1856-58), maintained a village not far from Tampa on the shores of Lake Thonotosassa. He was of the Mikasuki Seminole tribe and the Muskhogean family. The chief was deported in 1858 via New Orleans to the Indian Territory, where he died in 1859. Photograph from the Smithsonian Institution, Bureau of American Ethnology, from a daguerreotype copied by A. Z. Shindler in Washington, D.C., 1858; author's collection

Tampa owes its origin to the founding of Fort Brooke at the mouth of the Hillsborough River on January 20, 1824. The commanding officer of the military reservation was Colonel George Mercer Brooke. Photograph courtesy of Tony Pizzo

This scene of Fort Brooke, Tampa Bay, Florida, in 1837, was taken during the height of the Second Seminole War. Photograph from the author's collection

This tranquil view of the officer's barracks at Fort Brooke was taken during the last years of Fort Brooke. Seated on the verandah are several officers and a lady friend. The photograph is circa 1870s. Photograph from a stereo view by James C. Field from Florida Photographic Archives

Burying the hatchet after 150 years are these descendants of leaders on both sides of the Second Seminole War. Joe Dan Osceola, left, head of the Seminole tribe in Florida in 1974, greets Colonel and Mrs. George Mercer Brooke, Jr., at the Sesquicentennial Dinner of the Tampa Historical Society while local historian Tony Pizzo, second from left, joins in the fun. Colonel Brooke, professor of history at Virginia Military Institute, Lexington, Virginia, is a descendant of the founder of Fort Brooke. Photograph by Gary Rings, the Tampa Times, *from the author's collection*

Soldiers stand guard within the recently opened replica of Fort Foster, built in 1835 at present-day Hillsborough River State Park north of Tampa on U.S. 301. Fort Foster and its predecessor, Fort Alabama, were built to protect the bridge crossing on the Fort King Military Road, which led from Fort Brooke (now Tampa) to Fort King (Ocala). The fortification was named in honor of Lieutenant Colonel William Foster, who had reconstructed it. It was abandoned in 1838. Photograph courtesy of Florida Department of Natural Resources from the author's collection

Tampa's oldest dwelling is this one at 3210 Eighth Avenue, now owned by former City Judge Leo Stalnaker, Sr., a Tampa attorney. The house was built in 1842 by the grandfather of Dr. Sheldon Stringer and was erected on the site of the block where the city hall is today. Stalnaker's father, I. Stalnaker, bought and moved the structure in 1914 when the new city hall was started. The new address was in the town of Gary, a municipality for years. Photograph from the author's collection

This historic schoolhouse behind the University of Tampa is the proud showplace home of the DeSoto Chapter, Daughters of the American Revolution. The attractive frame structure was restored from the original, which was built in 1850 by General Jesse Carter. A native Floridian, Carter was one of the original trustees when Tampa was incorporated for the first time in 1849. He also had a contract to bring the mail in from Gainesville by stagecoach. Carter's daughter, Josephine, and her friends were the first pupils in the private school and a tutor was hired to teach them. Photograph by the author

Among the first settlers in Tampa were Levi and Nancy Dixon Coller, who came here in 1824 from North Florida. Levi was born in 1791 in Springfield, Massachusetts and died in 1855 in Tampa. In this photograph with him is his youngest daughter, Jeannette Coller Haskins (Mrs. W. T.), who was born in Tampa in 1841 and died here in 1935. The daughter gave an account of the family's early days to the Tampa Tribune *in 1914, reporting: "When the Coller family arrived here they found a bountiful country, with fish and game in abundance. Soldiers were under the command of Colonel George M. Brooke." Photograph courtesy of Jo Ann Haskins Cimino*

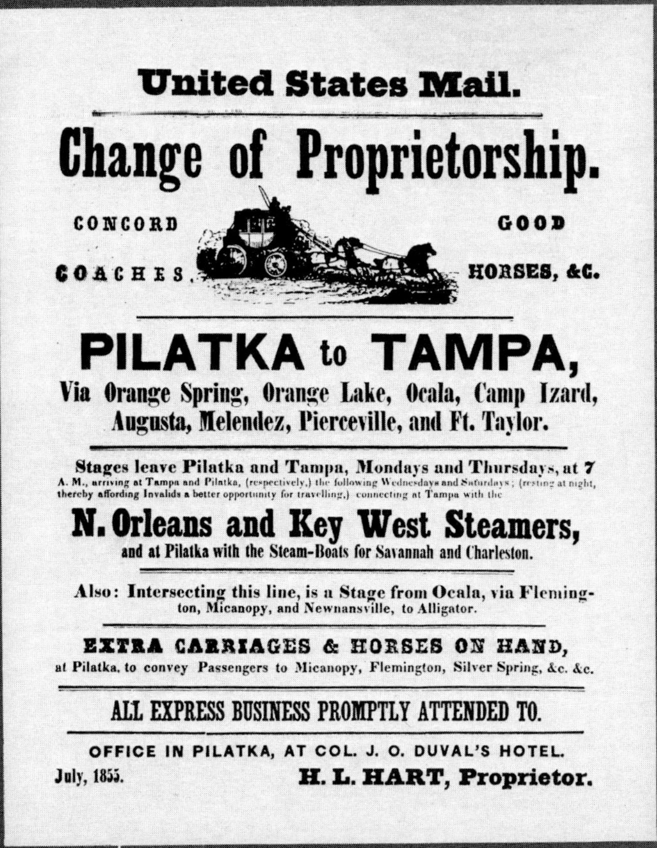
United States Mail.

Change of Proprietorship.

CONCORD COACHES, GOOD HORSES, &C.

PILATKA to TAMPA,

Via Orange Spring, Orange Lake, Ocala, Camp Izard, Augusta, Melendez, Pierceville, and Ft. Taylor.

Stages leave Pilatka and Tampa, Mondays and Thursdays, at 7 A. M., arriving at Tampa and Pilatka, (respectively,) the following Wednesdays and Saturdays; (resting at night, thereby affording Invalids a better opportunity for travelling,) connecting at Tampa with the

N. Orleans and Key West Steamers,

and at Pilatka with the Steam-Boats for Savannah and Charleston.

Also: Intersecting this line, is a Stage from Ocala, via Flemington, Micanopy, and Newnansville, to Alligator.

EXTRA CARRIAGES & HORSES ON HAND,

at Pilatka, to convey Passengers to Micanopy, Flemington, Silver Spring, &c. &c.

ALL EXPRESS BUSINESS PROMPTLY ATTENDED TO.

OFFICE IN PILATKA, AT COL. J. O. DUVAL'S HOTEL.

July, 1855. H. L. HART, Proprietor.

By 1855 Tampa was in touch with the outside world via overland stagecoaches. This poster advertises for passengers, mail, and express. Photograph from author's collection

The French writer Jules Verne (1814-1905) in his famous novel From the Earth to the Moon, *first published in 1865, chose Tampa as his launching site for the imaginary shot of his rocket to that planet. A century later, U.S. space projects including moon shots were being launched regularly from Florida, not too far away from what Verne called Tampa Town. A park at Ballast Point honors the French author. Photograph by the author*

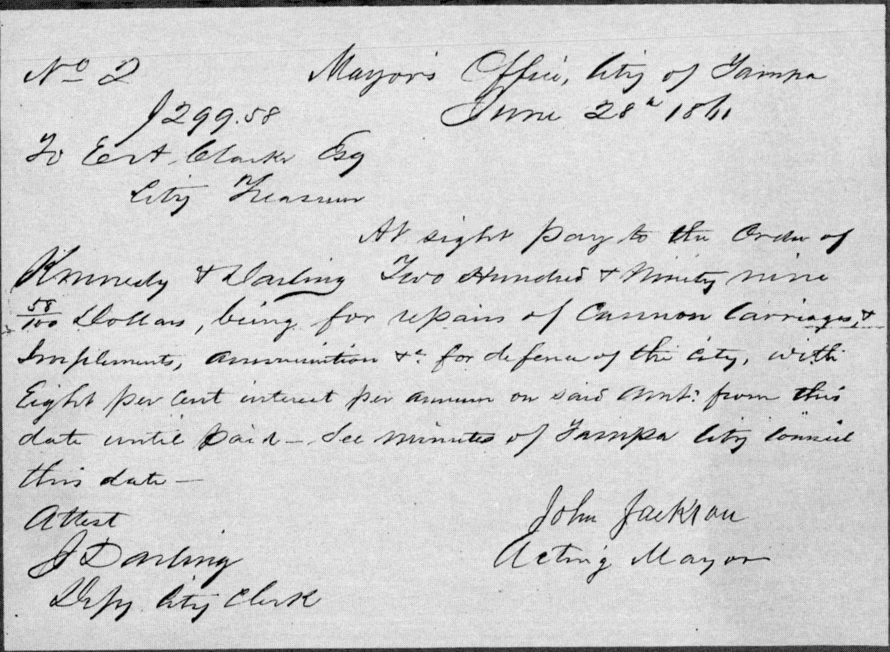
No. 2 Mayor's Office, City of Tampa

$299.58 June 28th 1861

To Ert. Clarke Esq

City Treasurer

At sight pay to the Order of Kennedy & Darling Two Hundred & Ninety nine 58/100 Dollars, being for repairs of Cannon Carriages & Implements, ammunition &c. for defence of the City, with Eight per Cent interest per annum on said Amt. from this date until paid— See minutes of Tampa City Council this date—

Attest

J Darling

Depy City Clerk

John Jackson

Acting Mayor

In June 1861 Tampa city officials were busy getting ready for the Civil War. Acting Mayor John Jackson issued a purchase order to Kennedy and Darling for $299.58 to pay for the repairs of cannon carriages and implements, ammunition, "etc." for "defence of the city." Photograph from the author's collection

William Ashley, a prominent white businessman and city official in the early days of Tampa, died in 1873 and was buried in Oaklawn Cemetery. Shortly after his death his black servant Nancy died. She was buried in the same grave with her master. Ashley's executor, John Jackson, erected a tombstone "to commemorate their fidelity to each other." The inscription reads: "Here lies Wm. Ashley and Nancy Ashley, Master, and Servant. Faithful to each other in that relation in life, in death they are not seperated (sic)*. Stranger consider and be wiser. In the Grave all human distinction of race or caste mingle together in one common dust." Photograph by the author*

Famed Southern poet Sidney Lanier (1842-1881) meditated as a winter visitor to Tampa in 1876, staying at the Orange Grove Hotel at Madison and East streets. He was inspired to write "Tampa Robins," "A Florida Sunday," and "The Mocking Bird," among other poems, while here. Lanier was a native of Macon, Georgia, and suffered from consumption, or tuberculosis. Photograph courtesy of the Greater Macon Chamber of Commerce, from the author's collection

The cultural center of Tampa in the 1880s, when this picture was taken, was the Branch Opera House on Franklin Street, near Lafayette Street (now Kennedy Boulevard), and opposite the old Hillsborough County Courthouse. The opera house was two stories high, with stores on the ground floor. The owner was Harry L. Branch, son of Dr. Franklin Branch. It was opened on March 7, 1884, when Lambert & Richardson's Dramatic Troupe presented the comedy Fate. *Next door to the south was the Emery, Simmons and Emery store, featuring "boots and shoes." Photograph from a stereo view by James C. Field, from the Florida Photographic Archives*

One of Tampa's earliest hostelries was the handsome Craft's Hotel. It looked like this circa 1870s. Photograph from a stereo view by James C. Field, from the State Photographic Archives

The pretty two-story house with wide verandahs sitting under giant, shady oak trees alongside State Road 60 in suburban Brandon has been a landmark for more than a century. It was built in 1876 by Jim Brandon, son of John and Martha Brandon who came to these parts in 1856 and settled with their eight children in a log house. A few years ago the historic structure was converted into a mortuary by Stowers Funeral Home. Photograph by the author

Dr. John P. Wall was an outstanding "mover and shaker" in Tampa in the 1880s. He was a noted physician; member of the State Board of Health; a founder of the Tampa Board of Trade; editor of the Sunland Tribune, *predecessor to the* Tampa Tribune; *and a natural-born civic leader. Photograph from the author's collection*

No vehicular bridges spanned the Hillsborough River in the 1880s. But there was this rickety pedestrian crossing at Jackson Street. A ferry-boat was available a block or so up-river. Photograph from the author's collection

The First Baptist Church of Tampa dates back before the Civil War, and seven Negro slaves and one free Negro were on the original rolls. The first house of worship was at Tampa and Twiggs streets, occupying "a lot given to the congregation by the County Commissioners for a Baptist church through the influence of Brother Martin Cunningham, who was then Clerk of the Circuit Court." This photo was taken in the winter of 1885-86 when the Reverend William H. Simons was pastor. The church subsequently moved to the west side of Hillsborough River and now is situated at Kennedy Boulevard and Plant Avenue. Photograph by James C. Field, from the author's collection

Tampa's steamboat wharf was humming with activity when this photograph was taken in 1882. The big vessel is the steamer Margaret *with Captain Randall the acting pilot. She was one of the Morgan Line fleet plying between here, Havana, Key West, and New Orleans. Tampa had a population of less than 600 at this time. Photograph by James C. Field, from the author's collection*

The Palmetto Hotel, built on the northeast corner of Florida Avenue and Polk Street (at right in this post-card view) in 1884 by Judge N. G. Buff of Terre Haute, Indiana, was one of the largest and most commodious hotels in South Florida. Built of wood, it had about forty rooms, was three stories high and had a five-story observatory. The sign on the building across the street reads "Hotel Le Fort." Postcard from the author's collection

The 109-foot motor schooner Dr. Lykes *was built in 1899 for Dr. Howell Tyson Lykes and Captain W. H. Towles of Punta Rassa for shipping cattle to Cuba. Also in the fleet was the little steamer* Fanita, *which had been built by the Vanderbilt family as a private yacht. Photograph courtesy of James M. Ingram, M.D., from the author's collection*

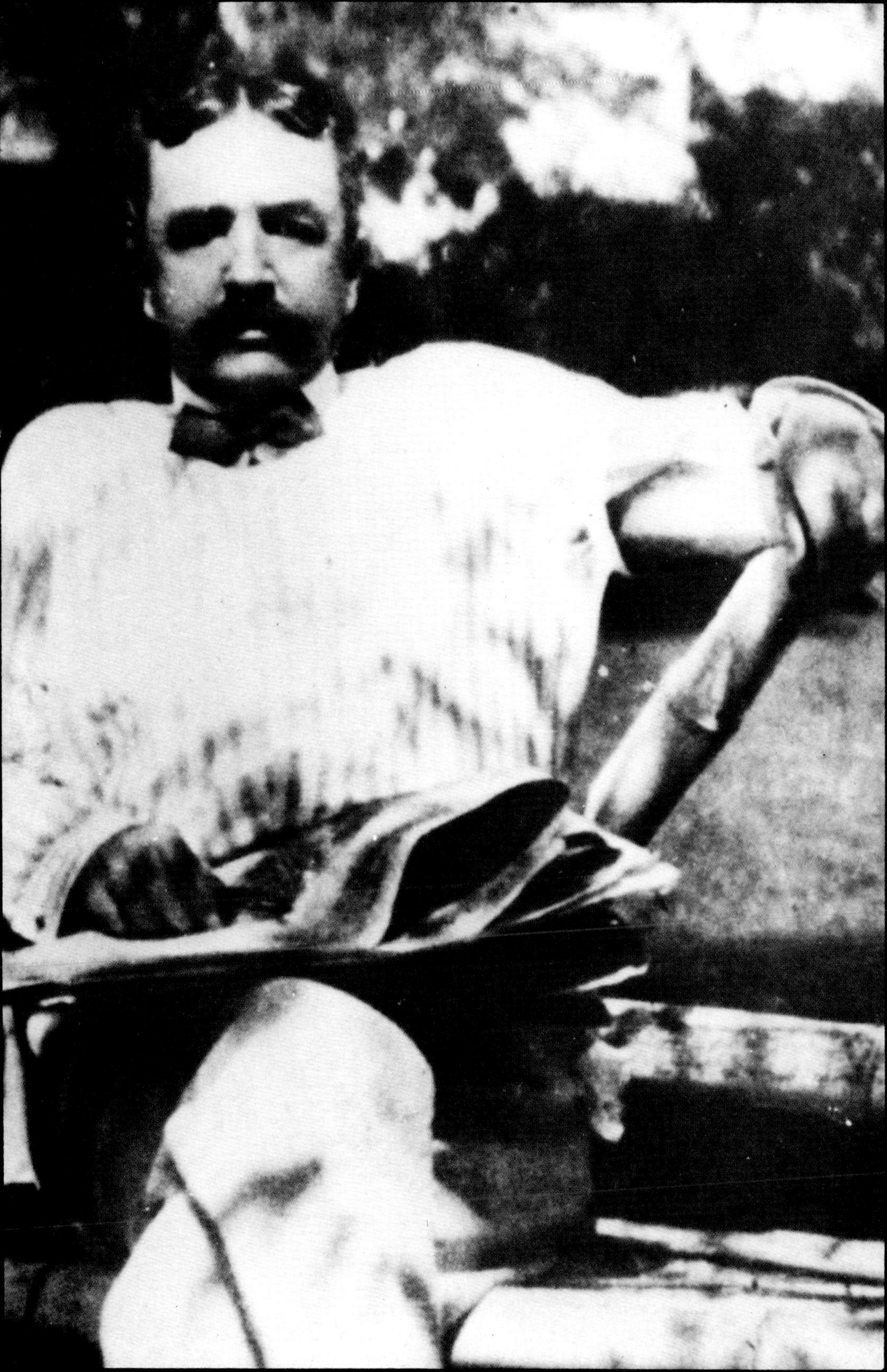

Dr. Howell Tyson Lykes, shown in this 1884 photograph, was a pioneer citizen of the Brooksville and Tampa areas. In 1874, when he was twenty-eight years old, he married Almeria Belle McKay, daughter of Tampa shipmaster and exporter Captain James McKay. They had eight children, a daughter and seven sons. Dr. Lykes not only was a physician, but he was a highly successful cattleman and shipper. Photograph courtesy of James M. Ingram, M.D., from the author's collection

The unique Tampa Bay Hotel was just opened for business, the city had just finished constructing the Lafayette Street (now Kennedy Boulevard) Bridge, and one of the first public parades was underway when this interesting photograph was shot. The magnificent hotel opened with a grand ball on February 5, 1891. Photograph by Conley and Company, from the author's collection

Henry B. Plant, a Connecticut Yankee, brought the railroad to Florida's west coast in 1884 and opened up the Tampa Bay area for development. He also built the fabulous Tampa Bay Hotel and other hostelries along the route of his excursion trains. Photograph courtesy of Frank Hutchins, from the author's collection

The Tampa Bay Galop, *composed by Jane Sarah Murphy (Mrs. J. M. Murphy), was copyrighted in 1890 just before the opening of Plant's elegant hotel. The dictionary defines Galop (or Galopade or Gallopade) as: "1. A lively dance in duple rhythm, popular in the 19th century; 2. The music for this dance." Photograph from author's collection*

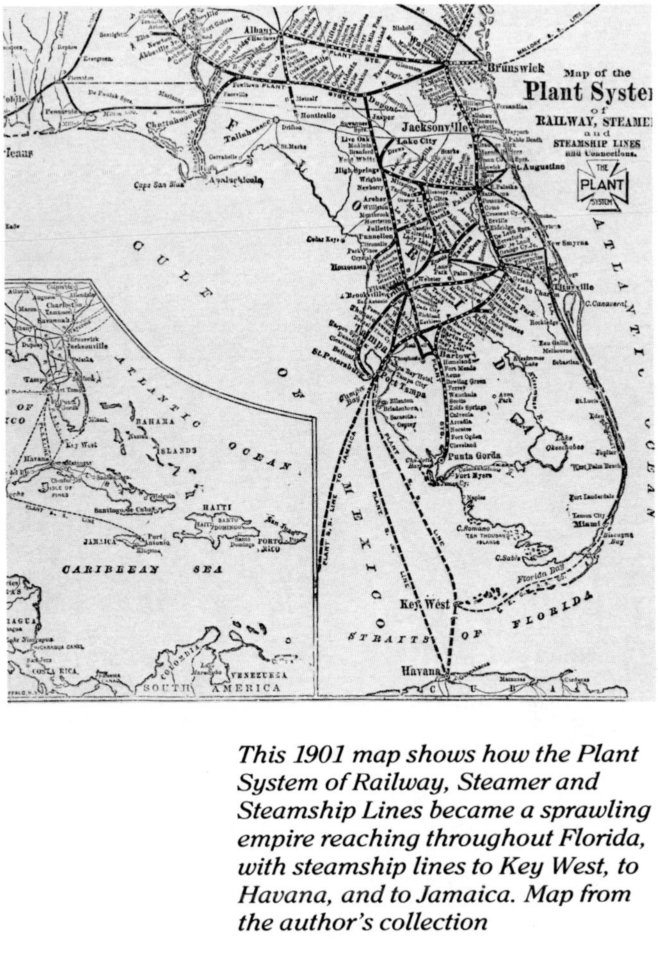

This 1901 map shows how the Plant System of Railway, Steamer and Steamship Lines became a sprawling empire reaching throughout Florida, with steamship lines to Key West, to Havana, and to Jamaica. Map from the author's collection

Henry B. Plant extended his railroad first to Port Tampa and there built his popular Port Tampa Inn right out on the docks. Guests could fish by throwing lines out of their windows. This picture was made in 1884 when everything was new. The guests seemed to be enjoying the boating. Photograph by the photographic studio of Ensminger Brothers, from the author's collection

This was downtown Tampa in 1885. That's the southeast corner of Franklin and Lafayette (now Kennedy Blvd.) streets, both avenues were unpaved but with trolley tracks running down Franklin. The corner building was known as Tibbett's Corner, where a confectionary store was operated for many years by the Tibbett Brothers. It was a Tampa landmark until the 1970s. Photograph by Burgert Brothers, from the author's collection

Henry B. Plant strikes a golfing stance for some of his guests at the Tampa Bay Hotel in this early photograph. The large woman in black in the center is Mrs. Plant. The man at far left is T. C. Taliaferro, prominent Tampan and founder of the First National Bank of Tampa. Photograph from the author's collection

Time was when every town that was any town at all boasted a cornet band. Our city formed the Tampa Silver Cornet Band in 1885 and it used to play music for events at the Branch Opera House on Franklin Street. A. A. Kelso, a skilled musician, was the organizer; C. E. Parcell, president; D. B. Givens, secretary; and C. W. Ayres, treasurer. Others in the original band were Fred Held, Charles Bailey, Adolph Stoy, Homer Hayden, Will Cline, Charles Scruton, P. R. Held, and Henry Kraus. When this photograph was made in 1890, some Lowrys had been added to the roster: Charles and Lafayette, third and fourth from right, and Samuel, seventh from right. Photograph from the author's collection

37
Plant System

The wood-burning locomotives huffed and puffed and provided power to pull the long trains of the Plant System. The railroad played an important role during the Spanish-American War of 1898, transporting troops to the port of embarkation at Port Tampa and thence by Plant steamship line to Cuba. Photograph from the author's collection

Ornate chandeliers and fancy iron grille guard the teller's counters made for handsome surroundings in the Exchange National Bank in 1894. Photograph by Burgert Brothers, from the author's collection

Though their uniforms were much different than today's, the members of Tampa's baseball team of about 1890 look slim and trim and ready for action. Fourth from the left is Samuel Lowry. Photograph from the author's collection

Sporting Stetson hats and neatly trimmed moustaches, these were Tampa's Finest—the police department around the turn of the century. J. C. (Jimmie) Jones was chief of police (second from left in front row with badge and "Chief" on his epaulet), who was with the department until 1930. Photograph from the author's collection

The Hillsborough County Courthouse was the gathering spot for Tampans after it was built in 1891. The handsome red brick structure occupied the block surrounded by Franklin Street, Madison Street, Florida Avenue, and Lafayette Street (now Kennedy Boulevard). It was designed by J. A. Wood, the same architect who planned the Tampa Bay Hotel. Band concerts and political speakings took place in the corner band shell. Postcard view from the author's collection

On March 16, 1890, almost four years to the day after the first cigar was rolled in Ybor City, the first mass was celebrated in the home of a Mr. Tissler on Sixth Avenue between Fourteenth and Fifteenth streets. By April of the following year the first Roman Catholic Church edifice was completed on Seventeenth Street and Tenth Avenue and named Our Lady of Mercy after the patron saint of Ybor City, Nuestra Señora de la Mercedes. Founder of Ybor City, V. Martinez Ybor, helped support the church. The property, 350 by 220 feet, was bought for $5,000 and was selected by Father de Carriere with a $1,000 down payment presented to Bishop John Moore by Henry M. Flagler, developer of the east coast of Florida. Other monies came from Tampa Jesuits, who for many years contributed all the personal alms they received and anything they could save. The first mass was said at 10 A.M. on April 19, 1891. The Reverend Achilles Vasta, S.J., a native of Italy, was brought to Ybor City in 1896 to this church. It was he who administered the Last Sacrament to Ybor. Ybor's widow, Mrs. Mercedes Ybor, donated the beautiful high altar to the church. Today the altar, the only remaining vestige of the historic old church, may be seen at the little St. Paul Church in Arcadia, Florida. The Ybor City church became known as Our Lady of Perpetual Help. Photograph from the author's collection

The honeymoon cottage of Colonel Peter O. Knight and his bride at 245 Hyde Park Avenue now is headquarters for the Tampa Historical Society. Knight was a prominent Florida lawyer, founder of the Tampa Electric Company and an outstanding civic leader. He came to Tampa in 1889 with his wife, the former Lillie Frierson. The house was erected in 1890. Photograph courtesy of the Tampa Historical Society, from the author's collection

Henry Laurens Mitchell was the first Tampan to be elected governor of Florida, serving from 1893 to 1897. A native of Alabama, Mitchell came to Tampa at the age of fifteen. He studied law and was admitted to practice in 1849, but he resigned as state attorney to enlist in the Confederate Army when the Civil War began and served as lieutenant and captain. At the close of the Vicksburg campaign he resigned to become a member from Hillsborough County of the 1864 Florida House of Representatives, to which he had been elected in his absence, and served again in both the 1873 and 1875 sessions. He was appointed to the state supreme court in 1888 and served until 1891, when he resigned to run for governor. After his term as the state's chief executive, he was elected clerk of the circuit court and then county treasurer of Hillsborough County. He died in 1903 at the age of 72 and is buried in Oaklawn Cemetery. Photograph from Florida State Photographic Archives, R. M. Strozier Library, Florida State University

Ybor City was a place of intrigue throughout the buildup to and duration of the Spanish-American War. José Marti, the leader of the Cuban insurrection, often visited Tampa to recruit volunteers from among the Latin cigar makers and others to go join the fight in Cuba. Marti was here as early as 1891 and before retiring the first night said, "I feel happy amongst warriors." Today, a José Marti Park is at Eighth Avenue and Thirteenth Street at the spot where Marti stayed at La Casa de Pedroso, the house of the great woman patriot of Cuba, Pauline Pedroso. Photograph by the author

This panoramic postcard issued about the turn of the century features the new Lafayette Street Bridge, the first vehicular span across the Hillsborough River. It also gives a good view of the city's waterfront, with the caption, "The Hillsboro (sic) *River and Bay offer splendid opportunities for manufacturing establishments. The waterfront, chiefly on the river, is used for warehouses and wholesale houses. The Lafayette Street bridge was erected in 1895 at a cost of $80,000." Lafayette Street now is known as Kennedy Boulevard. Photograph from the author's collection*

The U.S. Army staged for overseas duty here in Tampa during the Spanish-American War. Top brass included General Joe Wheeler, left, and General W. R. Shafter, conferring in one of the tent cities that spotted the area. Photograph by Parlow, Photographer, from the author's collection

These adventuresome volunteers for service in the Spanish-American War stopped off in Lakeland for a coffee break en route to Tampa. This was part of the Seventy-first Regiment, New York Volunteers. Photograph from the author's collection

An inscription on this big cannon reads, "This gun erected at Fort Dade for the Defense of Tampa in 1898." The piece is now on display on the campus of the University of Tampa. Photograph by the author

Tampa's main drag, Franklin Street, looked like this before the turn of the century. The caption on this old postcard boasts: "In addition to its superb hotels its reputation as a great winter tourist resort, Tampa points with pride to its thoroughly metropolitan public and private buildings, its excellent water system, its broad well-paved streets and its rapid transit facilities. It is often called: "The Magic City of The Gulf." In this scene Maas Brothers department store was well established—but on the east side of Franklin. The store was founded in 1890 by brothers Abe and Isaac Maas. The postcard comes from Mrs. Thomas Beusse and was written by Captain Jesse Hoyt Beusse to a good friend in Athens, Georgia. He was with the First Georgia Volunteers in the Spanish American War in 1898. Photograph courtesy of Mrs. Thomas Beusse, from the author's collection

Life in Tampa was rather dull for the troops awaiting transportation to Cuba. This chap gets a haircut while his buddies kill time watching. Photograph by Gibson Willets, from the author's collection

Frank D. Jackson, who was to become one of Tampa's most successful businessmen, was a cadet graduating in the class of 1896 from Florida State College at Lake City when this portrait was struck. FSC later became the University of Florida at Gainesville. Photograph courtesy of Richard D. (Dick) Jackson

During an unwelcome vacation from the front lines of the Spanish-American War, Clara Barton, founder of the American Red Cross, picnicked at the water's edge on the grounds of the Tampa Bay Hotel. This rare photograph was made by Miss Annie Laurie Dean and is one of the few known pictures of Miss Barton of this era. Miss Barton (striped neckpiece) is seated to the right of the coffee urn. The famed nurse was first stationed in the plush hotel but soon moved to more modest quarters on Plant Avenue. Photograph from the author's collection

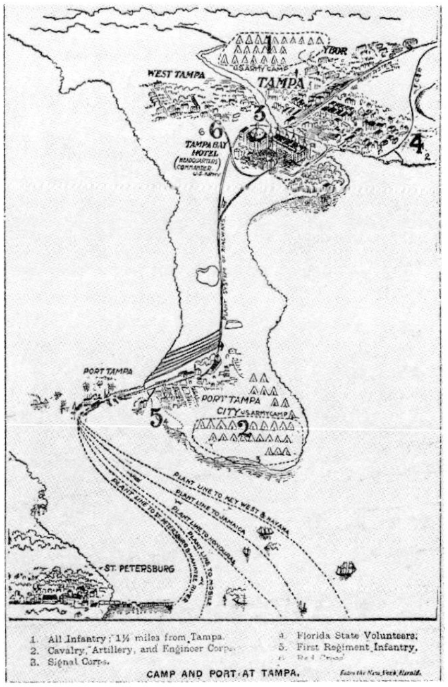

This map, published originally in the Tampa Daily Times *on June 21, 1898, shows sites of the U.S. Army camps here during the Spanish-American War. Headquarters for the high brass was at the elegant Tampa Bay Hotel. Other troops were billeted in tent cities throughout Tampa. Henry B. Plant's railroad and steamship lines were used to transport the army to Cuba. Photograph from the author's collection*

A gala officers' ball was a high social event at the elegant Tampa Bay Hotel during the Spanish-American War. A military band plays while ranking officers and their ladies stroll on the huge verandah. Photograph from the author's collection

There was no television or telephotos *or satellite pictures during the Spanish-American War, so metropolitan newspapers sent artists to the combat zone to record the scene for history. This drawing from a northern newspaper shows U.S. troops boarding ships at Tampa to embark for Cuba. The artist was identified only as "War Correspondent." The conflict became known as "The Correspondents' War" and it has been charged that William Randolph Hearst of the* New York Journal *and his rival Joseph Pulitzer of the* New York Journal *deliberately urged the country into war in their competition for higher circulation figures. Photograph from the author's collection*

A beautiful Tampa belle in 1898 was Miss Annie Laurie Dean, the subject of this lovely portrait. Photograph from the author's collection

HENRY
MERCHANT
KRUSE
TAILOR.

Chapter 2

1900 through 1919

The famous war correspondent, Richard Harding Davis, was in Tampa during the Spanish American War in 1898. He badmouthed our town in his writings, labeling it "a sand-blighted city."

It might have been considered as such in those days, but soon Tampa moved to take its place among the modern, progressive cities in the nation. Streets were brick-paved, trolleys were operating over the city, and water and sewer improvements were made. And the brilliant Tampa Bay Hotel was luring tourists here.

History was made here on January 1, 1914 when an intrepid pilot, Tony Jannus, successfully began the world's first commercial airline, a hop over the bay between Tampa and St. Petersburg.

World War I found Tampa to be a bustling city with humming shipyards turning out vessels for the war effort. The community was shocked when word was received that the U.S. Coast Guard Cutter U.S.S. *Tampa* was torpedoed and sunk in the Bristol Channel off England, carrying to a watery grave twenty-six Tampans.

At the end of the decade, our victorious soldiers had returned home from World War I and residents were looking forward to an era of "happy days are here again".

Merchant-Tailor Henry Kruse was in business on Lafayette Street (now Kennedy Boulevard) near Franklin Street back of Henry Giddens clothing store in 1904, and the tailors took a few moments out to pose for this picture. Photograph from the author's collection

The interior of a department store in 1903 is shown by the O. Falk and Brother store on the southwest corner of Franklin and Polk streets. Featuring clothing and shoes, it operated for many years, later as O. Falk's and finally as just Falk's. It closed in the 1970s. Photograph from the author's collection

The Egmont Key Lighthouse has been a sentinel in the dark at the entrance to Tampa Bay since 1848. The same year it was built a mighty hurricane struck the Gulf Coast and damaged the lighthouse, causing its keeper to resign his post. Ten years later a new eighty-five-foot tower was erected—the structure which still stands today. The once-kerosene-powered light is now a monstrous dual-light electric system that reaches out some twenty-two miles over the waters. In the olden days the lightkeeper had to trudge up eighty-five steps to get to the light and fire it up; today a simple switch at ground level does the trick. In 1939 the U.S. Coast Guard took over operation of the Egmont Key lighthouse along with others around the coastline from the U.S. Lighthouse Service. This photograph was taken on April 30, 1901. Photograph from the author's collection

Ladies of Sacred Heart Catholic Church were raising money for the building fund when they operated this fair or bazaar in the structure even before it was completed, about 1904. The marble columns, familiar to today's congregations, are visible in the picture. The woman at the left is Kate V. Jackson, and the woman in the big hat is Kate Carty (Mrs. T. V. R. Carty). The priest is the Reverend John Foulkes, S. J. Photograph from the author's collection

Come to the fair! This age-old cry has rung out since 1905, when the forerunner of today's gigantic Florida State Fair began in Tampa. It was a modest beginning as this rare photograph shows. The picture, handed down through the Brorein family (W. G. Brorein was "Daddy" and president of the Fair Association for many years), shows the ticket booth—50¢ please. The date was uncertain. Photograph from the author's collection

The old Bourquardez place at North Boulevard and Chelsea was country-like and "in the boonies" when this photograph was taken in 1905. The house was built in 1904 by pioneer Constant Bourquardez (Constant and Laurel streets are named for Mr. and Mrs. Bourquardez). The two-story frame structure was demolished in the early 1970s. It was across the street from Central Christian Church. The homestead was lived in by the late Robert Constant Bourquardez, who died in 1947, and his wife, who died in 1971. His nephew, Phil Bourquardez, was city clerk for many years. Photograph from the author's collection

At the turn of the century Tampa was but a sleepy little village. This brick building at the southwest corner of Florida Avenue and Lafayette Street (now Kennedy Boulevard) was quite adequate for the city hall and for the police and fire departments. It was built in 1890 at a cost of $10,000. This photograph was made in 1905. Photograph by Burgert Brothers, from the author's collection

Downtown Tampa was a busy place as this picture taken at the turn of the century depicts. It might have been a Saturday, the liveliest shopping day of the week. The scene is at Franklin Street and Lafayette Street (now Kennedy Boulevard), looking north with the courthouse square on the right. It appears to have been a scorching day, because most of the ladies had their umbrellas raised and the gentlemen wore hats. The Branch Opera House is seen at the left foreground. Immediately down the street is the First National Bank (with marble front and a flagpole visible). There was a double track for the trolley cars. Photograph courtesy of Mrs. Yetive Olson

Tampa's famous Gasparilla parade started off as a flower parade, a sort of small-town Rose Parade. This was a float in 1905 with Wordie Caldwell and Virginia Wood driving the swan. Photograph from the author's collection

Royal pageantry marked the coronation of the courts of Ye Mystic Krewe from the beginning. This photograph shows the crowning of the Royal Court of Gasparilla II. Included in the picture are (standing left to right) George Hardee, Walt Dorchester, Dr. Rollin Jefferson, Stella Long, Kathleen Phillips, King W. C. Gaither, Queen Mary Carnes, Helen Warner, Lillian Stevens, Craig Phillips, R. C. Carnes, Penn Dawson, and Charles Davis (kneeling in front). Photograph from the author's collection

Here are Kathleen Phillips, left, Queen of Gasparilla in 1910, and Mary Carnes, the second Gasparilla Queen in 1905. Photograph from the author's collection

Look pretty, girls, for our picture in the paper. All decked out in their finery, ladies of the Tampa Students Art Club pose for the photographer for the Tampa Daily Times, *which was getting up its summer edition. Photograph from the author's collection*

This troop of well-dressed, wide-awake salesmen traveled for J. R. Martin and Company and got about in this handsome rig, about 1905. Photograph from the author's collection

This diamond-shaped mounted photograph presents Mrs. Frederick J. James and little Lesley with a picket fence behind them. Photograph from the author's collection

"Tampa's worst fire," according to Tampa fire Department historian Lieutenant Edgar Gray, was the one that swept through a large portion of Ybor City on March 1, 1908. The hose wagon company stationed at No. 4 was the first unit to answer the auxiliary alarm at 9:33 A.M. The address was 1914 Twelfth Avenue, a two-story wood frame house used as a boarding house. The fire originated on the wooden shingles. In spite of valiant efforts of the fire crews, the flames grew larger and sparks ignited surrounding dwellings. It spread to engulf everything from Twentieth Street to Sixteenth Street and from Twelfth Avenue to Michigan Avenue (now Columbus Drive), a total of fifty-five acres. The five-hour blaze consumed 171 cottages, forty-two two-story frame buildings, five cigar factories, and five brick stores. Total damage was estimated at more than $1,000,000. Photograph courtesy of Reggie McAteer, from the author's collection

The Wilson Line's City of Philadelphia *was advertised on this postcard as "one of the fine steamers making the delightful trip through the beautiful Hillsboro* (sic) *and Tampa Bays and the Manatee River between Tampa, St. Petersburg and Bradentown" (now Bradenton). It was a popular excursion vessel in the first quarter of this century. Photograph from the author's collection*

Prominent Tampa sportsmen return February 23, 1909 after a big fox and wildcat hunt. The heavy gentleman on a horse in the center of the picture is Gordon Keller, well-known merchant and civic leader, who was leader of the hunt. Among his friends on the hunt was T. M. Wier. Photograph courtesy of Mrs. Sara Keller Hobbs, from the author's collection

A black shoeshine boy named Sambo was a favorite visitor to the downtown store of Gordon Keller (seated). That's Mayor F. L. Wing standing. The men's clothing store was at the southeast corner of Franklin and Lafayette streets. The bulletin board lists rental properties available in 1908. And what bargains! There's a "nice eight room house at 208 Palm Avenue for $21 a month," or how about a "nice five room cottage at 1518 Franklin Street for $18 a month"? Or perhaps a more modest six-room cottage at 807 and at 809 Ashley Street for $13 a month. Photograph courtesy of Sara Keller Hobbs, from the author's collection

The steamer Manatee, *shown in this photograph taken in 1909, was one of the best-known boats which ever plied the waters of Tampa Bay. It was operated by the Independent Line, headed by H. Walter Fuller, which became the Favorite Line. The lines in the area engaged in a steamboat war over rates. Photograph from the author's collection*

Another large load of hay is being hauled from the Atlantic Coast Line Railroad freight depot to the Miller-Jackson Grain Company on Ashley Street in 1911. The firm was founded in 1909 by R. W. Miller and Frank D. Jackson. In 1920 Jackson bought out his partner and the business name was changed to Jackson Grain Company. Photograph courtesy of Richard D. (Dick) Jackson

They looked like a clean-cut bunch of big bruisers, these guys on the 1909 Hillsborough High School squad having their picture made on the steps of the Tampa Bay Hotel. Fritz Bucholtz was the coach (extreme left in second row) with others in the same row, (left to right): Sam Gardner, Melvin Asp, Sumter L. Lowry, Jr., Frank Bowyer, Sim Sparkman, Dudley Towne, Kelly Jones, Galvin Elliott, and Jim Coarsey. In the front row (left to right) are: David Sherrill, Frank Winn, Stanley Asp, Bill Chambers, Captain Alec Shaw, Robert Nelson, Ray Shawl, and Theron Smith. Photograph courtesy of Mrs. Pat Turner

Meet the 1910-11 basketball squad of Hillsborough High School. And not a single one of the hoopsters are identified! Photograph courtesy of Mrs. Pat Turner

Tampa's second general strike in the cigar industry raged in 1910 and was climaxed by the fatal shooting of J. F. Easterling, a bookkeeper, when he was leaving the plant of Bustillo Brothers and Diaz cigar factory. Two Italians, Angelo Albano and C. Ficarrotta were suspected of being the murderers and were arrested in West Tampa, according to historian Karl H. Grismer. Sheriff's deputies arrived to take them to the county jail. Dramatically, a mob seized the suspects near Grand Central and Howard avenues, dragged them to a nearby oak grove, and hung them from a tree. This is a photograph of that scene. On December 28 a Grand Jury reported that it could not get any information regarding the identity of the mob members. The strike finally ended on January 26, 1911. Photograph from the author's collection

Isn't he a cute little fella? Meet Wilbur W. Meadows, son of the Reverend S. G. Meadows, indefatigable Methodist circuit rider who served rural Hillsborough County early this century. The Reverend Mr. Meadows first was pastor of the Riverview Methodist Church from 1912-14, then moved to the community in 1919, served again as pastor in 1923-24 and once more in 1937-38. Photograph by John C. Field, from the author's collection

Daredevil pilots thrilled crowds at the South Florida Fair in the early days of aviation. Here, Lincoln Beachey cavorts in the air while Jack Douglas McCurdy's plane sits poised on the track ready for a performance. This took place on February 19, 1911. The very next month Beachey was credited with making the first night flight by aircraft—again here in Tampa. And a few days later, McCurdy communicated the first wireless message from air to ground at Palm Beach. Photograph from the author's collection

A landmark in Sulphur Springs for many years was the interesting-looking Colonial Hotel, situated next to the springs. Photograph from the author's collection

In 1905 the Elks' Club purchased this private frame residence at Florida Avenue and Madison Street, to which splendid additions of white brick were made. The entire cost was reported to be about $17,000. The lodge was situated on the site of the homestead of pioneer Tampan Dr. John P. Wall and was opposite the Hillsborough County Courthouse. A large red brick building replaced this one in 1913. Subsequently, in the 1950s, the Elks' Lodge moved out on Bayshore Boulevard, taking over the old Crystal Ball Restaurant. Photograph from the author's collection

Tampa got a new tower annex to its historic city hall in 1979, but the attractive old building continued to serve the public. The original city hall is on the National Register of Historic Places. Built in 1914, the architects were Bonfoey and Elliott. The wedding cake structure is topped by a clock tower where Hortense the clock has kept generations of Tampans posted on time, sometimes not too accurately. The picture shows the building under construction. Photograph courtesy of "Salty Sol" Fleischman

The Tampa Automobile and Golf Club at Rocky Point was a popular spot for the younger set in 1913 when this photo was taken. This happy group was ready to tee off for an afternoon of pleasure. Left to right: Mrs. William Jackson; Mrs. Gertrude Wagner of Johnstown, Pennsylvania; Mrs. Kathryn Magnon; Mrs. Dora Bonacker Helms; and the next two are unidentified. Photograph from the author's collection

They were catching the big 'uns back in 1916. Frank D. Jackson, left, and J. L. Cone show off their trophies. Both were prominent Tampa businessmen. Photograph courtesy of Richard D. (Dick) Jackson, from the author's collection

Tampa's Captain Carnes, a Confederate veteran of the Civil War, was still spry and frisky in 1913 when he attended a reunion in Chattanooga, Tennessee. This photograph was taken at Craven's Farm on Lookout Mountain. Photograph from the author's collection

They also served, these front office employees of Ybor City cigar factory, No. 224, around the turn of the century. Note how well the young ladies and gentlemen are dressed. Photograph from the author's collection

On January 1, 1914 history was made in the Tampa Bay area when Tony Jannus inaugurated the world's first commercial airline. He flew his Benoit airboat between St. Petersburg and Tampa, a flight of twenty-three minutes. This photograph shows Jannus (in white pants and dark coat) with dignitaries as the crew prepares the craft for the inaugural trip. Seen standing on the other side of the fuselage at the cockpit is a crew mechanic, J. Leland Seale, who lives today in Port Charlotte. Photograph courtesy of J. Leland Seale

In World War I, as in World War II, Tampa was a busy shipbuilding center. This photograph shows the launching of a vessel at the Oscar Daniels Drydock Company. The name imprinted on the ship is Tampa. *Dignitaries doing the honors are decked out in their Sunday best. The press was there; note the press cards in their hats. The company had a contract to build ten 10,000-ton ships during the war. At the peak of the activity, 3,400 workers were employed. Photograph from the author's collection*

It was a day of great sorrow in Tampa. A stunned community had just received the appalling news of a week-old tragedy that wiped out the lives of two dozen young Tampa sailors along with 15 other Floridians. Making it even more shocking was the startling word that the city's own namesake vessel—the U.S.S. Tampa*—had been sunk in the faraway theater of war. At 8:45 P.M. on September 26, 1918 in the dark waters of England's Bristol Channel, an explosion was felt by lead ships in a large convoy. Just before that happened the U.S.S.* Tampa*, one of the escort ships, had slipped ahead of the armada for some unknown reason. Suddenly she became the target of the Huns' torpedoes! It is believed that this was the greatest single loss sustained by any community in the United States in World War I. Including the Floridians, the crew totaled 131. On March 19, 1981 a new U.S.S.* Tampa *was christened at ceremonies in Tacoma, Washington, with Councilman Helen Chavez officially representing the city. United States Naval Intelligence photograph, from the author's collection*

Patriotic parades were frequent in Tampa during World War I. Here, our doughboys come marching home on Franklin Street in 1918. The procession is making the turn at Lafayette Street (now Kennedy Boulevard). The marble front building flying the flag is the old First National Bank structure. Photograph by Burgert Brothers, from the author's collection

Tampa's famed Company H, 124th U.S. Infantry, got involved in the World War I conflict early, even before the big fighting began. The unit, put together by Sumter L. Lowry Jr., was formed in 1914 and saw immediate service on the Mexican border. They fought together there and later on in France. Here are the noncommissioned officers of Company H, photographed at Camp Wheeler, Georgia in November 1917. Back row, (left to right): Rondo Hatton, Will Davis, Harold McGucken, Eugene Richard, John Dekle, Gettis Henderson, and Joe Butzloff. Middle row: Kenneth McPherson, James Booth, George Sheldon, First Sergeant Byron Bushnell, Temple Hodges, and Carl Epping. Front row: Roy Frierson and Emil Fabian. Photograph from the author's collection

They went away smiling, these surviving members of Tampa's historic Company H after their farewell reunion dinner on November 7, 1980 at the Seville Restaurant. The group had held annual get-togethers, but no more. It became more burdensome every year to make the effort to go out socially. "Old soldiers never die," said General Douglas MacArthur, "they just fade away." Company H vets broke out the wine and celebrated their last reunion—and then just faded away. Left to right: Herbert Gray, John Forsythe, Emil Fabian, Lieutenant General Sumter L. Lowry (their commander from the beginning), Joe Butzloff, Ed Olsen and Ralph Rouse. Photograph by the Tampa Times, *from the author's collection*

Lieutenant General Sumter L. Lowry, with steady hand, gently pours a glass of rare wine as he readies a farewell toast to his men of Company H at their final get-together in 1980. Lowry, who died February 3, 1985, at the age of 91, led the unit through all its years since its formation in 1914. The wine was donated in 1923 and had been carefully stored for the day when the final survivors would get together and fade away. Photograph by the author

This quartet of young blades became prominent Tampa businessmen. The snapshot, taken in 1919, presents (left to right) Raymond Fleming, Richard D. (Dick) Jackson, Roland A. Wilson II, and Harold Wolf. Photograph courtesy of Richard D. (Dick) Jackson

Colleen Moore grew up in Tampa—fast. In 1917, at the tender age of 15, she went to Hollywood and made it big. Not as a child star, but as the first movie flapper. She appeared in her first film, The Bad Boy, *that very year. The winsome beauty with one brown eye and one blue eye was to become the number one box-office attraction in 1926 and 1927. Colleen, born Kathleen Morrison, lived in Hyde Park near the Bayshore and was a pupil at the Convent of Holy Names, then located on Twiggs Street. (It's now the Academy of Holy Names on Bayshore Boulevard). Among her classmates were Sophia S. Earle, Edith Gibbons, Edith Allen, Marie McKean, and Rosa Galvin. Her favorite teacher, she revealed years later, was Sister Ignatius, who was the music teacher. This photograph shows Colleen third from the right in front. "My peers and I were all more interested in* Photoplay *magazine than in Latin," Colleen wrote in her autobiography,* Silent Star. *She and her friends kept scrapbooks of their favorite stars, and Colleen left a blank page in her album—for herself when she became a star! Photograph courtesy of Sophia S. Earle, from the author's collection*

Here's a publicity still of Colleen Moore in her first movie, The Bad Boy, *made in 1917 when the Tampan was only fifteen years old. She played a soubrette, a city girl who tries—and fails—to woo a bucolic young man away from his country sweetheart. Colleen's uncle in Chicago had pull in Hollywood and got her a screen test. Photograph from the author's collection*

This is Colleen Moore early in her screen career. "I was the spark that lit up Flaming Youth," wrote F. Scott Fitzgerald, "Colleen Moore was the torch. What little things we are to have caused all that trouble." And acid-tongued movie critic George Jean Nathan once wrote: "To those who believe Colleen Moore is a greater actress than Greta Garbo, I say you go to your church and I'll go to mine." Photograph from the author's collection

Movies starring Colleen Moore were great attractions in her hometown of Tampa for more than a decade. This advertisement appeared in the Tampa Daily Times *on April 25, 1929. Note the "sexy" language in the text of the ad. Advertisement from the author's collection*

When Colleen Moore was a highly paid superstar, she put together a fabulous dollhouse—a fairy castle that took seven years and almost $500,000 to build. She took it on a nationwide tour in 1938 to raise one million dollars for crippled children. One of the stops was in her hometown of Tampa where the doll house was displayed at Maas Brothers. The marvelous miniature mansion was nine feet square and twelve feet high. Its fittings and furnishings were the most luxurious and costly imaginable; diamonds and rubies, emeralds and other precious stones, largely Miss Moore's personal jewelry. Platinum, gold, silver, onyx, and crystal all were used lavishly in its furnishings and construction. This is a photograph of the living room. Featured by a diamond and pearl chandelier, decorated with emeralds, and containing the world's smallest electric light bulbs the size of grains of wheat, the living room attracted world-wide attention. A rose quartz floor and Cinderella murals by George Townsend Cole are highlights in this bewildering by beautiful room which is furnished with golden and silver tables, a carved ivory piano, and the smallest chess table in the world. The dollhouse today is on permanent display at the Chicago Museum of Science and Industry. Photograph from the author's collection

The bustling intersection of Franklin and Madison streets is seen in this photograph, circa 1920. The handsome marble front of the First National Bank glistened in the sun. An elderly gent shuffled out to get on the Woodlawn streetcar. Beckwith-Range Jewelry, Giddens Clothing Store, and the Bay View Hotel are also in sight. Photograph from the author's collection

Chapter 3

1920 through 1929

The era from 1920 through 1929 was one of the liveliest in the history of Tampa.

The decade started off with the reorganization of city government, and from 1920 to 1927 the community operated under a city manager system. Municipal services were improved and many capital improvements were made.

Tampa suffered one of its most devastating storms in 1921 when a vicious hurricane struck on October 25. The barometer dropped to 28.81, wind gusts exceeded 100 miles an hour, 6.48 inches of rain fell in a 24-hour period, water rose 10.5 feet above mean low tide, 50 feet higher than in any other hurricane since the big gale of 1848. Trolley cars and tracks were wrecked along Bayshore Boulevard and the steamboat *Pokonoket* was beached on the grounds of the Tampa Bay Hotel.

George S. Gandy opened Gandy Bridge in 1924, a toll bridge which provided a direct link to St. Petersburg.

The dizzying Florida real estate boom electrified Tampa the same as other areas of the state. Speculators poured into town and real estate sales zoomed. Many developments were built. D. P. Davis dredged up three small isles near downtown Tampa and developed Davis Islands, a swank residential section from the day it opened, and it still is today. The Municipal Hospital was moved to the Island and opened in 1927.

With the advent of prohibition, a new industry—bootlegging—thrived and speakeasies dotted the city.

The happy days came to a sudden halt with the collapse of the real estate boom, the crash of Wall Street, and the closing of the Citizens Bank and Trust Company and other banks in the community.

Tampans did not panic or flee town; they got set to brave tough economic times and to carry on toward recovering the good living to which they had become accustomed.

The Tampa cigar industry suffered another general strike in 1920, which did not end until early in 1921. The strikers held a mass meeting "celebration" on October 14, 1920 in the Centro Asturiano Theatre to mark six months of the dispute. A total of 7,613 union men quit work, all the cigar factories closed, and 3,500 persons were thrown out of work. Photograph courtesy of Dr. Gary Mormino, University of South Florida

The worst hurricane Tampa experienced since the terrific storm of 1848 struck the Tampa Bay area on October 25, 1921. Heavy rainfall accompanied the high winds; more than 6.48 inches of rain came in twenty-four hours. This was the scene in Suburb Beautiful in Tampa's exclusive Bayshore District on October 25. Photograph from the author's collection

Solemn ceremonies marked the dedication by the Rotary Club of Tampa of Memorial Highway at Howard Avenue and Grand Central Avenue (now Kennedy Boulevard). The dedication, on January 2, 1921, honored the Hillsborough County men who lost their lives in World War I. The monument at this intersection became a traffic hazard in the late 1930s and was removed to the area in front of the American Legion Cemetery at Dale Mabry Highway and Kennedy. Photograph by C. Verne Klintworth, courtesy of Evanell K. Powell Brandt

Many a violator rode this "taxi" to the local calaboose in the 1920s. The police patrol wagon, affectionately known as "The Black Maria," is parked in front of police head-quarters, then located behind city hall on Jackson Street and Florida Avenue. Photograph by Burgert Brothers, from the author's collection

This is the real Sulphur Springs the way it looked on a happy day in 1922. The refreshing waters had not become so commercialized then, but it was a popular swimming hole never-theless. Photograph by the Burgert Brothers, from the author's collection

This trio of lovelies modeled the latest bathing costumes and competed for beauty honors at Ballast Point in 1922. Dig those boots on the doll in the center! The Ballast Point Pier could be reached from anywhere in town by streetcar for only a five-cent fare. Photograph by Burgert Brothers, from the author's collection

Tampa had its own close-in beach for a period during the 1920s. It was called Sunset Beach and was on the bay about where present-day Culbreath Isles development on West Shore Boulevard is. This picture was made during the Fourth of July celebration and beauty contest in 1923. Photograph by Burgert Brothers, from the author's collection

Spooning couples in 1922 found canoeing on the Hillsborough River in the vicinity of Sulphur Springs to be not only relaxing—but romantic as well! Photograph by Burgert Brothers, from the author's collection

Tampa was shocked and saddened on February 21, 1922 when news reached the city of the crash of the army airship Roma *at Norfolk, Virginia. It was being piloted by Captain Dale Mabry, World War I hero from Florida. This is a picture of the crew of the ill-fated craft. Front row, left to right, Captain Walter J. Reed, Major John G. Thornell, and Captain Dale Mabry. The enlisted men in the rear row are not identified. A number of Mabry's relatives live in Tampa today. Photograph courtesy of Ben Goldman, Langley Air Force Base, Hampton, Virginia, from the author's collection*

Here is the Roma *being moved from her hangar at Langley Air Force Base in 1922 just before the crash that took the life of Tampa's Captain Dale Mabry. The airship was bought from Italy and had been retrofitted with powerful Liberty engines. The increased power caused the semirigid nose section to collapse and the big craft, with a crew of forty-four fell to earth over Willoughby Point in Norfolk. Miraculously, ten persons survived the crash. But Captain Mabry's body was found badly burned and with his hands on the wheel. In Tampa, Dale Mabry Highway, built during World War II to connect MacDill and Drew Air Fields, was named in his honor. Photograph courtesy of Ben Goldman, Langley Air Force Base, Hampton, Virginia, from the author's collection*

Offered here is a grand view of three important public buildings as they appeared in 1922. At left is the Elks' Lodge at the corner of Florida Avenue and Madison Street. In the center is the Hillsborough County Courthouse, and at right in the rear is the Tampa City Hall. The scene is looking southeast from the intersection of Franklin and Madison streets. Only the city hall stands today, and a tall annex has been built adjacent to it (on the site where the Hendry and Knight Building is seen here). The city hall is listed on the National Register of Historic Places. Note the loafers enjoying the benches around the courthouse. There also is the band shell where concerts and political speakings were held. Photograph by Burgert Brothers, from the author's collection

As early as 1923, when this photograph was shot, professional baseball teams trained at Tampa's Plant Field on North Boulevard. The sports facility was a part of the layout of the Florida State Fair. This property now has been transferred to the University of Tampa. The Cincinnati Reds trained here for many years. Photograph by the Burgert Brothers, from the author's collection

"Watch Us Grow!" was the slogan of the Victory National Life Insurance Company the day it opened for business on November 5, 1923 in this small building on Marion Street just south of Lafayette Street (now Kennedy Boulevard). And grow it did. Later it became the mammoth Gulf Life Insurance Company. Victory National was capitalized for $500,000, this being the only life insurance company organized in Florida at the time, by Florida men and with Florida capital. The entire operating staff that opening day is shown in this picture (left to right): Loper B. Lowry, sales force; Marjorie Giles Davis, policy writer and stenographer; Sumter L. Lowry, president and general manager; and D.S. Hull, actuary. Photograph from the author's collection

The Italian Club staged a gigantic picnic on May 18, 1924 to encourage a membership drive. Philip F. Licata was president. A string band was on hand to provide music, Boy Scouts were there to assist in handling the crowds, and a good time was had by all. Several Anglo-Saxon dignitaries attended, including D. B. McKay, former mayor of Tampa and publisher of the Tampa Daily Times*; Colonel Peter O. Knight, attorney and president of Tampa Electric Co.; and State Representative (later Circuit Judge) Harry N. Sandler. Photograph courtesy of Dr. Gary Mormimo, University of South Florida*

The gang's all here. The crew at Tampa Fire Department Station No. 2, Twelfth Street and Columbus Drive, posed for a portrait in 1924. Captain T. G. McAteer, third from left in back row, was on the force thirty-three years before retirement in 1932. He died in 1952. Standing next to him (second from left, back row) is Fred Dreves, then driver, who later became fire chief and fire marshal. Photograph from the author's collection

This is how a professional architect's office looked in 1923. It is believed this was the office of Fred J. James, who designed many public buildings in Tampa. Photograph from the author's collection

Gandy Bridge, connecting Tampa with St. Petersburg, was opened with fanfare on November 24, 1924. These are just a few of the dignitaries (left to right): Governor Clifford Walker of New Jersey, one of 16 visiting governors; Miss Sara Lykes Keller—then Miss Tampa, later Mrs. W. Frank Hobbs—who helped to cut the ribbon; and D. P. Davis, the developer of Davis Islands. The span originally charged tolls, which were taken off during World War II. Photograph from the author's collection

The so-called Biglow Mansion at Bayshore and Gandy boulevards of late is being restored and turned into a modern housing development. But when this photograph was taken it was a private clinic known as Bayside Hospital. The original owner, Silas L. Biglow, was a well-known businessman and politician in Tampa at the turn of the century. He moved to his mansion in 1908. Dr. John S. Helms purchased the rambling structure from Biglow's widow in 1917 to be used as a residence. By 1919, the physician had added a northern wooded frame addition and converted the mansion into a hospital. Dr. Helms was widely respected in the community. He was chief of staff and director of surgery at Bayside, which was recognized as one of the best-equipped hospitals in the country. He also was one of the founders of the present Tampa General Hospital, which moved to its present location on Davis Islands in 1927. When the municipal hospital opened, Dr. Helms converted the Biglow mansion to its original residential use. Dr. Helms died in 1932. The building has been nominated to the National Register of Historic Places. This photograph shows Dr. Helms on the steps and his hospital staff. Photograph courtesy of Adalaide Bloch Morris

A fair is no fair at all without a colorful, noisy, fun-loaded, free-wheeling, hot-dog smellin' midway. And the South Florida Fair had that and more during its 1924 showing. The exposition later was to become the Florida State Fair. Photograph by Burgert Brothers, from the author's collection

The first singing commercials were aired here in Tampa over WDAE, Florida's first radio station. In 1925, this trio was called The Southern Songsters (left to right): Edith Price Montgomery (Mrs. M. L.), Sue Jones Klintworth (Mrs. C. Verne), and Georgia Goodell Rogers (Mrs. Nat). They sang a catchy little tune for Dodd Motor Company that began, "Buy a little Ford and ramble right along, park it on the Bayshore . . ." Station WDAE went on the air on May 15, 1922, one of the first broadcasting stations in the country. Photograph by C. Verne Klintworth, courtesy of Mrs. Evanell K. Powell Brandt

An overflow crowd of auto race fans who could not cram into the grandstand at the South Florida Fair in the early 1920s stood on the walkways surrounding the dirt track. The exposition building in the background is Wall Hall, named in honor of Mayor Perry G. Wall. Photograph by the Burgert Brothers, from the author's collection

Time was when steamboats were the main means of transportation for getting from here to there in the Tampa Bay area. One of the most popular vessels was the Pokanoket, *shown loading happy passengers in 1926. This was one of the boats run by the St. Petersburg Transportation Company, headed by H. Walter Fuller, and it ran from Tampa to Pass-a-Grille. Her nickname was the Poky Noky. Photograph by Burgert Brothers, from the author's collection*

Oldsmar, a village straddling the Hillsborough-Pinellas counties line, had its beginning in 1917 when Ransom E. Olds, pioneer automobile manufacturer of Lansing, Michigan, came into possession of 37,500 acres of land situated on Old Tampa Bay. The inventor and manufacturer of one of America's first automobiles, the Reo, from his initials, later named the Oldsmobile, envisioned a city around his newly founded motor plant. More than 1,000 Lansing neighbors shared his vision and moved their homes and families to the infant Oldsmar, planning to settle their land for generations. Bathing beauties helped to publicize Oldsmar (photo) *during the Florida boom in the 1920s; here was a trademark pointing to the town as the suburb to two cities—Tampa and St. Petersburg. After the collapse of the boom, Oldsmar lay dormant for several decades but now is making a comeback. The Tampa Bay Downs horse track is located here. Photograph from the author's collection*

Tampa got a taste of professional football way back in 1925 when Red Grange and his famous Chicago Bears played an exhibition game. That was during the Florida real estate boom and promoters of Tampa Beach latched onto them and hauled them out to their development. Of course, you remember Red—the immortal 77 and Galloping Ghost of the University of Illinois in his college days. Grange is still promoting real estate—he lives at and boosts neighboring Indian Lakes Estates in Polk County. Photograph from the author's collection

D. P. Davis Properties hauled 'em by the busloads, prospects to buy into his new development during the real estate boom. This fleet of buses, bearing the banner of "Davis Islands—Tampa in the bay," rushed buyers to the dredged-in property in the bay at the mouth of downtown Tampa. The lots sold like hotcakes and the Davis Islands project turned out to be one of the finest residential sections developed here during the boom. Lots selling for a total of $1,028,200 were sold on the first day of activity! Photograph courtesy of Ronnie Kolwak, from the author's collection

Meanwhile, elsewhere in the city other developments were blossoming even as Davis Islands was jumping. In the northeastern suburbs, the community of Golden Hills, Uptown Tampa was getting underway. It later became known as Temple Terrace and featured many orange groves. (It was here that the delicious Temple orange was developed.) This photograph shows Thonotosassa Boulevard, a narrow, red brick road with little traffic. The highway is known today as Busch Boulevard, one of Tampa's busiest streets, and it leads to Busch Gardens. Photograph by Burgert Brothers, from the author's collection

Soon after D. P. Davis opened his Davis Islands community, it became the scene of delightful Florida living. There was a golf club and a tennis club, and the lady residents whiled away many an afternoon batting the ball and the breeze. Photograph by Burgert Brothers, from the author's collection

Pretty as a picture was this interior of a fashionable Tampa home in 1926. This was the residence of José S. Franco at 2501 Watrous Avenue. Franco was owner of the Franco Drug Store at 1510 East Broadway. The designer of the handsome dwelling was Paul I. Parslow of the firm of F. D. Parslow and R. B. Gambier, Associate Architects. Photograph by Boozer and Rodgers, from the author's collection

Coming on the heels of the Scopes Trial in Tennessee in 1925, a bill was introduced in the 1927 Florida Legislature to prohibit the teaching of evolution in public schools. Sponsor of the measure was Representative Leo Stalnaker, Sr., of Tampa, shown in this photo taken in the 1960s. He's holding a headline reading HOUSE PASSES APE BILL from the Tampa Daily Times *during the 1927 session. The bill passed the Florida house by a sixty-seven to twenty-four majority but failed to clear the Florida senate before adjournment. The controversy grabbed headlines all over the country. Stalnaker, still practicing law in Tampa and in his 80s, today believes his bill was "a good one." Photograph by the author*

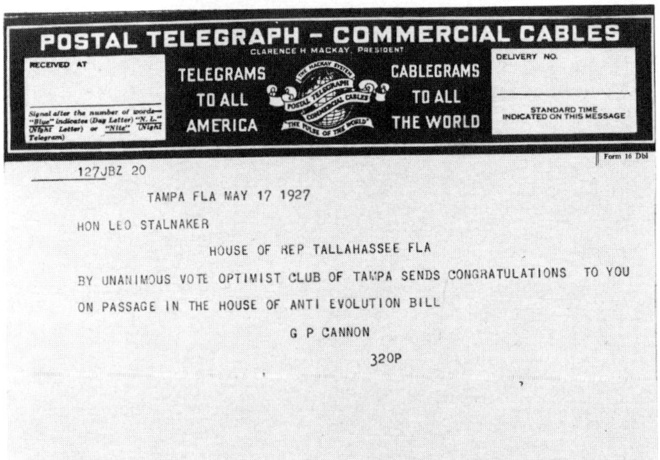

POSTAL TELEGRAPH – COMMERCIAL CABLES

CLARENCE H. MACKAY, PRESIDENT

TELEGRAMS TO ALL AMERICA — CABLEGRAMS TO ALL THE WORLD

127JBZ 20

TAMPA FLA MAY 17 1927

HON LEO STALNAKER

HOUSE OF REP TALLAHASSEE FLA

BY UNANIMOUS VOTE OPTIMIST CLUB OF TAMPA SENDS CONGRATULATIONS TO YOU ON PASSAGE IN THE HOUSE OF ANTI EVOLUTION BILL

G P CANNON

320P

Tampa's Representative Leo Stalnaker, Sr., received widespread support for his anti-evolution bill in the 1927 legislature. The Optimist Club of Tampa sent him this telegram via the old Postal Telegraph service. A man in DeFuniak Springs wrote: "If there are any monkeys or apes in the legislature they ought to be unseated, but of course you cannot tell who they are as some of them resemble a man so much but after the vote is taken then you can tell by their vote who are the monkey's descendants." Photograph from the author's collection

After his term in the legislature, Leo Stalnaker, Sr., was municipal judge of Tampa. He's shown presiding over the notorious Key Club Case on November 8, 1927. The courtroom was jammed for the proceedings. Photograph from the author's collection

ATLANTIC COAST
HOTEL HILLSBORO
MAAS BROS

This excellent skyline view of Tampa was shot from the Tarr Furniture building (later Seminole Furniture) in June 1927. It's looking east across the Lafayette Street (now Kennedy Boulevard) Bridge with the dome of the First Baptist Church in the near right. The Atlantic Coast Line Railroad freight depot was where the Curtis Hixon Convention Center and parking garage are today. The Tampa Terrace Hotel, only a year old then, is seen in the distance across the bridge and opposite the city hall. The skyline as it looked then has been virtually wiped out, and in 1985 a new skyline featuring glass skyscrapers was forming. Photograph by Burgert Brothers, from the author's collection

Citrus groves thrive in the Tampa area. Here is seen the harvesting of a large orange crop in the 1920s. Photograph by Burgert Brothers, from the author's collection

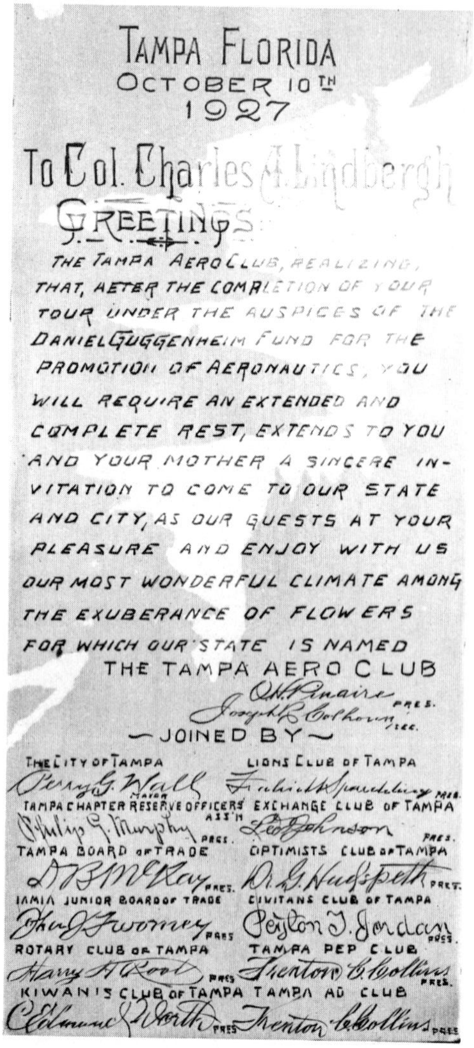

TAMPA FLORIDA
OCTOBER 10TH
1927

TO COL. CHARLES A. LINDBERGH

GREETINGS:

THE TAMPA AERO CLUB, REALIZING, THAT, AFTER THE COMPLETION OF YOUR TOUR UNDER THE AUSPICES OF THE DANIEL GUGGENHEIM FUND FOR THE PROMOTION OF AERONAUTICS, YOU WILL REQUIRE AN EXTENDED AND COMPLETE REST, EXTENDS TO YOU AND YOUR MOTHER A SINCERE INVITATION TO COME TO OUR STATE AND CITY, AS OUR GUESTS AT YOUR PLEASURE AND ENJOY WITH US OUR MOST WONDERFUL CLIMATE AMONG THE EXUBERANCE OF FLOWERS FOR WHICH OUR STATE IS NAMED

THE TAMPA AERO CLUB

O. H. Pinaire PRES.
Joseph L. Colhoun SEC.

—JOINED BY—

THE CITY OF TAMPA	LIONS CLUB OF TAMPA
Perry G. Wall MAYOR	PRES.
TAMPA CHAPTER RESERVE OFFICERS ASS'N	EXCHANGE CLUB OF TAMPA
Philip G. Murphy PRES.	Leo Johnson PRES.
TAMPA BOARD OF TRADE	OPTIMISTS CLUB OF TAMPA
D. B. McKay PRES.	Dr. G. Hudspeth PRES.
TAMPA JUNIOR BOARD OF TRADE	CIVITANS CLUB OF TAMPA
PRES.	Peyton T. Jordan PRES.
ROTARY CLUB OF TAMPA	TAMPA PEP CLUB
Harry H. Root PRES.	Trenton C. Collins PRES.
KIWANIS CLUB OF TAMPA	TAMPA AD CLUB
PRES.	Trenton C. Collins PRES.

After Colonel Charles A. Lindbergh's thrilling conquest of the Atlantic Ocean in May 1927, just about every community in the country wanted the hero to visit their town. Tampa was no exception. The Tampa Aero Club, with O. H. Pinaire as president, prepared a scroll invitation that was signed by presidents of every major service club in the city urging Lindbergh and his mother to come spend a while here. Lindbergh never visited Tampa, but he did get into Jacksonville and Miami. Photograph by Burgert Brothers, from the author's collection

"Roque in Tampa, Florida, in December" is the apt title of this interesting picture taken in the 1920s. The game was being played on courts at the Tampa Tourist Center behind the Tampa Bay Hotel (now University of Tampa). Note the gentlemen all had hats and coats on and the ladies were equally well dressed. Photograph by Burgert Brothers, from the author's collection

During the 1920s social events took place at the Tea Garden and Jewel Box in Plant Park on the grounds of the Tampa Bay Hotel. A postcard view of this event was captioned: "During the warm days of summer and winter this is an excellent place to spend an afternoon and evening. It is beautifully decorated and entirely surrounded with masses of natural foliage." Photograph by Burgert Brothers, from the author's collection

For three winter seasons during the 1920s, Colonel Harold B. Bachman and his Million Dollar Band played concerts in Tampa's Plant Park. Thousands of Tampans and winter visitors turned out for the Sunday events, which also were broadcast over radio station WDAE. During World War I, Bachman was band leader of the 116th Engineer Band which played overseas, where one general said his music was "worth a million dollars" to his men. The band also played at Palm Beach during the winters and in the summers traveled the U.S. on the Chautauqua circuit. Bachman also served in the army in World War II. In 1948, he took over the Fightin' Gator Band of the University of Florida. Photograph from the author's collection

This quartet of winsome lassies was in a playful mood when along came the photographer and snapped the beach scene. He forgot to get their names. Photograph from the author's collection

Here's Franklin Street looking south from Polk Street on a typical day in June 1927. There was a double trolley track and automobiles were parked parallel as traffic had increased during the boom days. The Tampa Theatre, billed as "The South's Most Beautiful Theatre," had just opened a few months before and the Franklin Theatre was doing good business across the street. The Citizens Bank and Trust Company in the tall skyscraper at right, was considered a strong financial institution at the time but collapsed in 1929. Photograph by Burgert Brothers, from the author's collection

Don't Spend It All!
CITIZENS BANK AND TRUST CO.
TAMPA
The Franklin Theatre
FRANKLIN
MAAS BROS.
O. Falk's
DEPARTMENT STORE
EVERYTHING TO WEAR
FOR MEN WOMEN & CHILDREN
Burgert Bros
Tampa
V1452

Bayshore Baptist Church itself was brand new when its Sunday school got together to pose for this photograph on April 11, 1926. The church was organized on March 29 of that year. The pastor was Dr. George Hyman. The building was at Dekle, Howard, and DeSoto avenues. Photograph by Boozer and Rodgers, from the author's collection

For many years L. M. Hatton, Sr., was the dedicated president of Tampa Business College. A student, Bernice Dunn, snapped this picture of the educator in 1927 at the college on Lafayette Street (now Kennedy Boulevard) and Edison Street. Hatton's son, L. M. Hatton, Jr., also was on the staff and in 1928 was elected sheriff of Hillsborough County. Photograph courtesy of Mrs. Bernice Dunn Lilley, Dunnellon, Florida, from the author's collection

Ahh, for a nice spring day and a Sunday joy ride with your best girl! In the 1920s, Memorial Highway, the road between Tampa and Clearwater, was a favorite for spooning couples. They could pick the colorful blossoms of the oleanders or take pictures. It didn't matter where you parked your flivver; there wasn't enough traffic to be a problem. By this time, the oak trees and other landscaping planted by the Rotary Club of Tampa in 1921 when the highway was dedicated were coming along just fine. Photograph by Burgert Brothers, from the author's collection

This picture shows but a few of the hundred thousand persons who witnessed the first Southeastern Air Meet held at Tampa on February 22, 1928 on the occasion of the formal opening and dedication of Drew Field. Photograph from the author's collection

A nightmare spread over Tampa in May 1927 after a drug-crazed man wiped out the family of Mr. and Mrs. Herman Merrill, killing both parents and three of their children. A mob determined to lynch confessed murderer Benjamin Franklin Leavine stormed the Hillsborough County Jail for several nights but failed to get their man. The 116th Field Artillery National Guard, under command of Colonel Sumter L. Lowry, Jr., and Lieutenant Colonel H. W. Hesterly, restored law and order but not before five persons in the mob had been killed. Meanwhile, funeral services were planned for the victims. This photograph shows a section of the crowd of thousands of the curious who passed into a dimly lighted room of the B. Marion Reed Funeral Home on 916-918 Tampa Street at the corner of Tyler to view the bodies of the five Merrills. At one time the throng was so great the visitors went through the room at the rate of sixty-three a minute. Scarcely any of them knew the Merrills. Photograph by Boozer and Rodgers, courtesy of James E. Lawhon, from the author's collection

When the new Hillsborough County Jail was opened at 1301 Pierce Street in May 1926, it was claimed by officials to be "the most modern county prison in the South." The sturdy brick structure cost $350,000 and housed 344 prisoners. Fred J. James was the architect. Sheriff L. M. Hiers was the county's top law enforcement officer at the time. The jail at Jefferson and Pierce streets had not been occupied a year when its walls were tested and found to be "mob-proof." Lynch-minded mobs tried to enter it and steal a man accused of killing a family of five in May 1927. The leading news magazine of the time, the Literary Digest, *reported on June 18, 1927: "Battered by a huge stick of timber hauled to the scene by a truck and handled by fifty members of the mob which sought to lynch a confessed murderer, and its windows riddled with bullets, the Hillsborough County Jail nevertheless held off the besiegers although they returned to the attack three nights in succession." The jail was replaced in the 1970s by another "modern county prison." Photograph by Burgert Brothers, from the author's collection*

The crowds queued up to cram into the Victory Theatre to see Show Boat *one night in the late 1920s. The motion picture theater, at the northwest corner of Tampa and Zack streets, boasted Vitaphone, the new all-talking movies. In fact, a large sign bragged the Victory was "The Home of the PERFECT Talkies." Photograph by Burgert Brothers, from the author's collection*

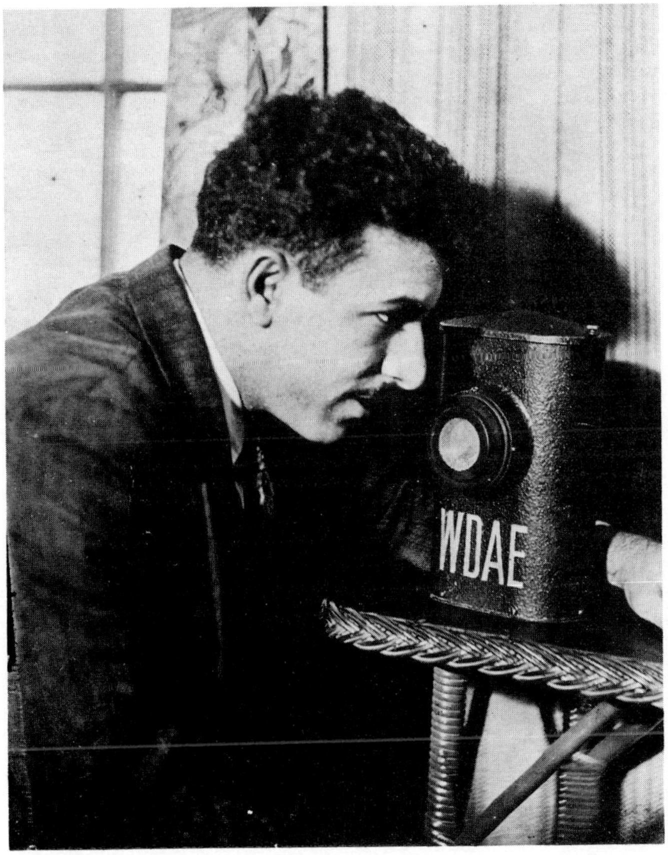

Sol Fleischman truly was an institution in broadcasting in the Tampa Bay area. Radio itself was young when Sol began as an announcer on station WDAE, Florida's pioneer radio station owned by the Tampa Daily Times. *The photo shows the handsome young man broadcasting over the first electronic microphone in 1928. Fleischman was an all-around announcer but gained fame as a sportscaster. He stayed on WDAE until 1957 when he moved over to television station WTVT. His career spanned nearly half a century. He retired a few years ago and now resides in Sun City Center and on Anna Maria Island. Photograph from the author's collection*

They first dreamed of a highway to connect Tampa and Miami back in 1914, before World War I. But it was not until 1928 that the dreamway became reality. Construction of the Tamiami Trail took fourteen years and cost more than $6 million—some say as much as $13 million. A three-day celebration marking completion began on April 24, 1928. The first event was a big shindig at Tampa's Municipal Auditorium with speakers being Governor John W. Martin (who had run on a platform calling for modern highways in 1924), Mayor D. B. McKay, T. Ed Bryan, W. W. Trice, and W. G. Brorein. This photograph shows a group of spectators looking over the progress during construction of the highway. It shows some of the difficulties the contractors met in building through the muck, mosquitoes, and alligators. Photograph from the author's collection

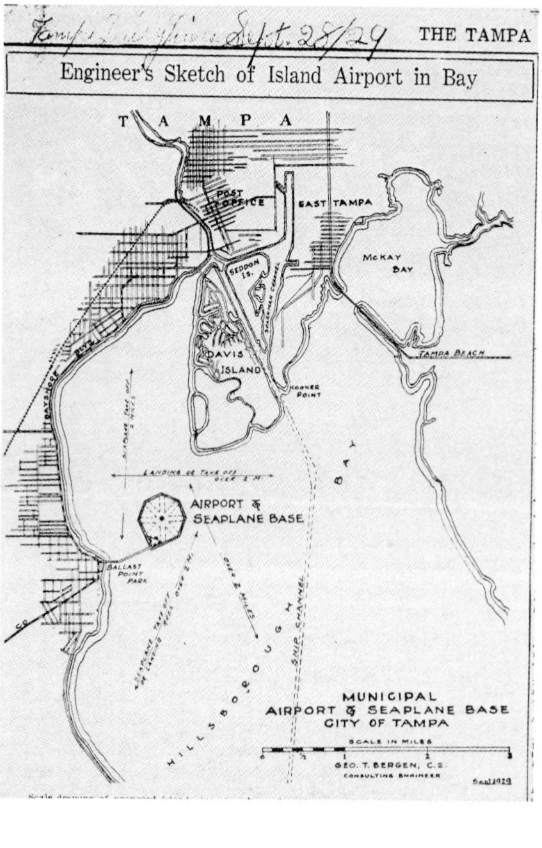

Tampa was embroiled in a terrific rhubarb in 1929 when it was proposed to dredge up an airport and seaplane base off Ballast Point. The demands for a first-class facility that would be available to both hydroplanes and land planes were inspired by promises from officials of the New York, Rio and Buenos Aires Airline (NYRBA), predecessor of the Pan American Airways, that Tampa would be made the base of operations for the company if such an airport were provided. Tampa voters approved a $750,000 bond issue to finance the port. Then came the eruption of a community-wide fight. Many residents along Bayshore Boulevard, the city's most fashionable neighborhood, got up in arms opposing the project, saying it would lower their property values. The politicians and civic leaders also debated the plan. One civic leader pushing the project was Jerome A. Waterman, Maas Brothers department store official, a pilot and aviation enthusiast. Appearing before the city council, Waterman predicted that commercial flying would soon be done largely in big flying boats carrying from fifteen to fifty persons. Plans for the island airport finally were shelved and Pan American abandoned in disgust the idea of establishing its base in Tampa and went to Miami in January 1930. Photograph of map in the Tampa Daily Times, *from the author's collection*

Daredevilry provided amusement for Tampans at the end of 1929 as banks were closing and the stock market was crashing. This photo taken October 12, 1929 shows flagpole sitter Richard Blandy ascending the pole atop the tower of Pioneer Tire Company at Tampa and Whiting streets. Blandy was originally scheduled for eight days—but stayed up twenty-eight days! The promotion gimmick attracted crowds throughout his stay. Photograph by Burgert Brothers, from the author's collection

In the gloomy days of 1929, just as the stock market was about to crash and Florida's real estate boom already had collapsed, Inspiration Pictures, a company of more than 100 persons from Hollywood, swooped into Tampa to make a film. It was the first all-outdoor, all-talking picture ever produced, and it was called Hell Harbor. *The location for the filming was Rocky Point. Henry King, famed Hollywood director (who was married to a Tampa woman) was the director of the film which starred a Latin bombshell from South America, Lupe Velez. It also featured a local personality—Rondo Hatton, a reporter for the* Tampa Tribune. *Tampans hoped that this would be the first of many movies to be filmed here. Governor Doyle E. Carlton, a Tampan himself, wrote Henry King: "I am very glad that your organization used Florida as a setting for your recent production, 'Hell Harbor.' I am sure that the beauty spots of the State, the long hours of daylight, and delightful weather conditions peculiarly fit Florida for motion picture work." A few years later, Rondo Hatton was featured in Robert L. Ripley's "Believe It or Not!"* (photo). *Photograph of cartoon in the* Tampa Daily Times, *from the author's collection*

ARCH
TAMPA
CUT-RATE DRUGS
HALE DRUG CO.
J.M.MERRITT, PRES.
CUT-RATE DRUGS
PRESCRIPTIONS
HALE DRUG CO.
KODAKS-CANDY
NO PARKING

Chapter 4

1930 through 1939

The nationwide Depression of the thirties engulfed Tampa as it did the rest of the nation. There were widespread unemployment, soup lines, WPA projects, hard times.

But life went on. Handed a lemon, the city turned it into lemonade by selecting worthwhile improvement projects for the WPA: constructing the Peter O. Knight Airport, its handsome administration building, and a new National Guard Armory; rebuilding the seawall and Bayshore Boulevard; reroofing the Tampa Bay Hotel; developing new city parks, community buildings, and libraries; and performing other good works.

One of Tampa's own beauties, Margaret Ekdahl, became Miss America—1930.

In 1931, Tampa Junior College started as a night school in the Hillsborough High School building, then moved in 1933 to the vacant Tampa Bay Hotel and became the full-fledged, four-year University of Tampa. In 1934 National Airlines was born in the Tampa Bay area and eventually became a worldwide air service before merging with Pan American Airways.

Davis Causeway (now called Courtney Campbell Parkway) was built as a toll facility by Captain Ben T. Davis in 1934.

But, as the decade ended, there was good news and bad news for Tampa. The good news was that the shipyards were reactivated and MacDill Air Force Base was established. The bad news was that war clouds were hanging heavily over the United States and worldwide.

(overleaf)
The Great Depression was on and times were hard in the early part of the 1930s, but the one bright spot in town was the brilliantly-lit Tampa Theatre on Franklin Street. On this particular evening, Mae West and Cary Grant were starring in I'm No Angel. *After seeing the show, young couples dropped next door for a soda at the Hale Drug Company, run by J. M. Merritt. Professional offices filled the upper floors of the theater. A sign on the window reads, "Dr. J. R. Powell, Dentist." Photograph from the author's collection*

This group of well-dressed, grim-faced men composed the Detective Bureau of Tampa's Police Department in May 1930. Photograph by Burgert Brothers, from the author's collection

The main drag of Ybor City—East Broadway (now Seventh Avenue)—looked like this on a day in the early 1930s or late 1920s. The decorative iron grille on the balconies of the store buildings gave an attractive Latin look. This was the 1600 block. Photograph from the author's collection

The Red Mill was a swingin' place for young Tampans throughout the 1930s and 1940s. It was a restaurant and night club on Platt Street at Packwood and was operated by Lou Figueredo. This picture was taken in 1930. Photograph by Burgert Brothers, from the author's collection

Rockers lined up in military precision on the second floor verandah await guests of the Sulphur Springs Hotel and Arcade on a day in September 1930. The porch overlooked busy Nebraska Avenue. The hotel, originally called the Nebraska Hotel, was built in the 1920s by the late Josiah Richardson, developer of Sulphur Springs for years. The shopping center in the arcade brought national attention when Robert L. Ripley featured it in his "Believe It or Not!" cartoon as the only city under one roof. It had a drug store, grocery, shops of all kinds, and one could even get drunk in the shopping center—and be arrested, too—because the sheriff had an office here. The post office also had a branch. The arcade was torn down in 1975, over protests of history-lovers, to make way for a parking lot for the adjoining Tampa Greyhound Track. Photograph by Burgert Brothers, from the author's collection

She was modeling and selling bathing suits at Maas Brothers department store. And her wholesome, Swedish good looks and stunning figure made her a natural to compete in beauty contents. And so it was, Margaret Ekdahl—her friends called her "Mickey"—swept the Triple Crown of the world of pulchritude and became Miss America—1930. Before copping the national title she had been named Miss Tampa and Miss Florida. Thus, she went down in the record books as Tampa's, and Florida's, first and only Miss America. She dazzled audiences in many of the forty-eight states and was the toast of the nation. After her term expired, she came back to Florida but to Orlando, where she sold cosmetics in a department store. She was about ready to go to Sweden to make a film when tragedy struck. She suddenly developed appendicitis, and the appendix ruptured. She was rushed to an Orlando hospital—but help came too late. The misty-eyed Mickey, then only twenty years old, died. Photograph by Burgert Brothers, from the author's collection

This quartet of prominent Tampa Democrats was plugging for a New Deal in 1932. Mayor R. E. L. Chancey, wearing the light suit, donated to the party fund for a front license plate boosting Franklin D. Roosevelt for President and Dave Sholtz for governor. The gentleman at the left is unidentified. To the right of the mayor are Frazier T. Blount and City Attorney Alonzo B. McMullen. Hillsborough County went for FDR by a five-to-one margin. Chancey himself had just been elected in 1931 in a hotly contested campaign. The picture was taken in front of city hall. Photograph by Burgert Brothers, from the author's collection

Francis Bellamy, author of the Pledge of Allegiance to the Flag, worked and lived in Tampa in his sunset years. He had written the pledge in 1892 when he was editor of Youth's Companion *magazine. He came to this city in 1924 and became the first advertising manager for the Tampa Electric Company. A native of New York State, he died here in Tampa in 1931 at the age of seventy-five. He is buried in Rome, New York. In 1975, a new school at 9720 Wilsky Boulevard was dedicated as the Francis Bellamy School. The architect decorated the exterior with stars and stripes and an excerpt from the pledge. Photograph from the author's collection*

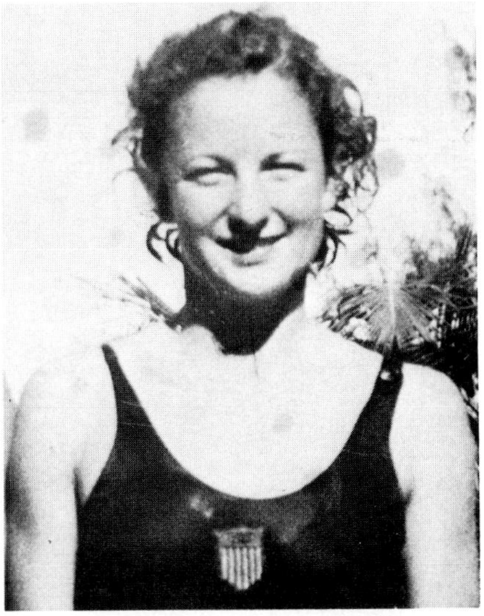

The Associated Press reported in a book, A Century of Sports, *that "the premier swimmer of the past among girls might well be Katherine Rawls. She won 33 national championships in the 1930s and was the first woman to represent her nation in the Olympics as both a swimmer and diver in 1932 and 1936." And this spectacular young athlete splashed into the world of competition right here in Tampa. Katy had learned how to swim in a fish pond—at the age of two—in St. Augustine. Then her family moved to a lake in Tampa. Her father was William Jennings Bryan Rawls. Another hero book,* Famous American Athletes of Today, *written by Harold Kaese and published in 1938 at the height of Katy's career, reported that "it was . . . in Tampa that Katy's ability first became the object of approval by other than members of her family and admiring friends." On Christmas Day, 1924, they opened a new swimming pool at Temple Terrace. Little Miss Minnow, as she was sometimes called, was only seven but she was fearless and talented and versatile. Throngs cheered as she dived from the twenty-five-foot board. The family later moved to Fort Lauderdale. Katy attended Florida State College for Women (now Florida State University) in the late 1930s. Photograph from the author's collection*

A favorite hangout for young folks especially was Falor's lunch stand and cool drink fountain at 3119 Florida Avenue. It was established in 1927 and was famous as the home of Falor's Triple XXX Root Beer. The spreading oak trees shading the building and parking lot made a cool place to stop on the hottest summer day, and in the wintertime guests were invited to have sandwiches and hot drinks in the lunchroom near the fireplace. This photograph was made in 1932 when Mr. and Mrs. Clyde Downs managed the business. At that time Falor's boasted as an attractive feature that it had a radio for entertainment of the customers. Photograph from the author's collection

The Goody Goody was family-owned from 1929 when William B. Stayer bought the place from Ralph Stevens, who had opened the Goody in 1925. Their butterscotch pie is rarely duplicated. Ann McDuffie, food editor for the Tampa Tribune, *says that the recipe, or one like it, is "unavailable." The menu once painted on the wall of an adjacent building is gone now, with its message: "Welcome to Tampa, Florida. Our people come from all over the world. Pioneers long ago with vision and sacrifice ordained the building of this city. Here you will find rest, strength, new hope and courage. Tampa is the gateway to the west coast of Florida." This interior scene was photographed on a busy day in February 1941. The Goody Goody was closed in May 1984—but for only a few months. It was reopened in January 1985, by Yvonne Freeman, who had been a waitress there for twenty-five years under previous owners. Photograph by Robertson-Fresh, from the author's collection*

Several generations of hungry Tampans have feasted on the delicious sandwiches, pies, and other goodies at the Goody Goody Sandwich Shop, 1119-21 Florida Avenue, which stayed in business until August, 1984. According to Evanell K. Powell in her Tampa That Was: *"The first drive-in east of the Mississippi—the 'Goody Goody' is one of the rare places where the looks have not been altered, nor has the quality of the food. While the piecrust is now prepared by the cooks, it was, until the last decade, always secretly made by the managers." This photograph was made February 18, 1932. Photograph from the author's collection*

The elegant Tampa Theatre continued to run a first-class showplace throughout the turbulent times of the Depression years. Management ran all kinds of gimmicks to pull the crowds and got results. There was bank night, with top prizes of automobiles. And there were bingo and screeno and vaudeville. The theater had its own symphony orchestra. And it had Eddie Ford—what an organist! He was brought on with a fanfare, and his $50,000 mighty Wurlitzer and he would be lifted on a rising stage with Eddie tickling those ivories. House lights were out, and multicolored spotlights were on the star. He was a showman and got the audience in a receptive mood to enjoy the first-run movie that was to follow. An unforgettable character he, Eddie Ford! This picture was taken on January 19, 1933. Photograph by Burgert Brothers, from the author's collection

Dr. Frederic H. Spaulding, first president of the University of Tampa, unlocks the main door of the world-renowned Tampa Bay Hotel building on August 2, 1933. The once-elegant hotel was now dedicated by civic spirit to the cause of education. Dean John Coulson of the university faculty looks on. The university had been founded as the Tampa Junior College in 1931 and held night classes at Hillsborough High School. When the institution moved to Plant Park, it became a full-fledged four-year University. Photograph by the Tampa Daily Times, *from the author's collection*

Three more freshmen students arrive at the University of Tampa on September 18, 1933 just in time for the first formal assembly of students in their new home at the old Tampa Bay Hotel. They are, from left to right: Fred Blackburn, Tampa; Bill Marbourg, Winter Haven; and Jack Godwin, Tampa. Photograph by the Tampa Daily Times, *from the author's collection*

When the University of Tampa was but an infant in 1933, the kids whipped up a great deal of campus spirit in a short time. There always was a lot of hazing and high jinks going on. Here, Willie Godwin, a freshman Spartan football player, submits to a belting from upperclassmen, left to right: Hasus Castro, W. C. Buchanan, and an unidentified student. Photograph by the Tampa Daily Times, *from the author's collection*

The sharpshooting Tampa Police Department won many medals and trophies during the national pistol championships at their home range in September 1935. One officer recognized is C. A. "Smitty" Brown, kneeling at extreme right in front row. Photograph from the author's collection

For many years before World War II, Tampa's excellent Police Pistol Range was the site for the national pistol championships. This photograph shows some of the crowds that came to watch the shoot-outs. Photograph from the author's collection

For many decades long freight trains hauling phosphate from the Polk County mines rumbled through downtown Tampa en route to Port Tampa where the loads were shipped from elevators onto freighters and sent to foreign ports. At one time there were five elevators used for the loading of phosphate. Number 1 and Number 2 elevators were built of wooden construction in 1893 and 1894. Others were added and in 1925 Number 5 elevator, shown in photo, was built of steel and was operated by steam until 1928, when it was converted to electrical power. The first vessel to load at this elevator was the General Wheeler, *a five-masted schooner. In June 1970 the Seaboard Coast Line Railroad announced that the phosphate elevator at Port Tampa was closed due to an unspecified "structural failure" and would not be reopened. The railroad then opened a new 12-million-ton-per-year phosphate loading facility, called Rockport, in the East Bay area. In January 1971 six Caterpillar tractors hooked onto old Number 5 and pulled it down—thus a mighty landmark tumbled to the ground. Photograph by Burgert Brothers, from the author's collection*

An engineering triumph was the completion of the Davis Causeway toll span across Old Tampa Bay between Clearwater and Tampa. It was the vision and dream of Captain B. T. Davis and was opened to traffic on June 28, 1934, just 10 years after an earlier span between Tampa and Pinellas County—Gandy Bridge, also a tollway—had opened. This aerial view shows the Tampa end of the nine-and-a-half-mile facility. The radio tower is that of WFLA, and the station's engineer, Joe Mitchell, lived in one of the houses in the foreground. After World War II, during which the causeway was taken over by the federal government and the tolls lifted, Davis Causeway was renamed Courtney Campbell Parkway. Campbell was a member of the old state road department and later, as congressman, worked to get the approaches improved and to erect roadside parks. Photograph from the author's collection

This was the tollgate on the Clearwater side of Davis Causeway. The Davis family lived in quarters over the gate. Tolls were fifty cents round trip for passenger cars and all passengers. Photograph by Burgert Brothers, from the author's collection

This is Captain Ben T. Davis, the builder of Davis Causeway. Although the span he constructed during the Depression days has since been named Courtney Campbell Causeway, Davis's name is perpetuated in the Ben T. Davis Beach, a City of Tampa recreation spot on the east end of the causeway. Photograph courtesy of George Davis, from the author's collection

For amusement, Tampans went to the dogs during the Depression years of the 1930s. Here's an early view of the Tampa Greyhound Track. From the looks of the crowd, the track must have had a good handle that day. Photograph by Burgert Brothers, from the author's collection

A major airline was born in the Tampa Bay area during the depth of the Great Depression in 1934 by the awarding to National Airlines of a 142-mile mail route between St. Petersburg and Daytona Beach, via Tampa, Lakeland, and Orlando. The first flight was on October 15. The "fleet" consisted of two second-hand Ryan aircraft. The airline had five employees, including George T. (Ted) Baker, the dauntless and persevering architect of National Airlines, who is shown in the picture (in shirtsleeves) of a group beside a ten-passenger Stinson that the company was proudly displaying at the time in 1936. The plane cruised at 130 MPH. Photograph from the author's collection

Pretty stewardesses had been a trademark of National Airlines since its early days. National flourished for many years and its flights were extended to many parts of the world. But, finally, in January 1980, the Tampa-Bay-born airline was merged with Pan American. Photograph from the author's collection

TAMPA MORNING TRIBUNE

42ND YEAR—NO. 247 TAMPA, FLORIDA, WEDNESDAY, SEPTEMBER 4, 1935 PRICE FIVE CENTS

65 MILE WIND WHIPS CITY
CHANCEY LEADS BY 3702

STORM PASSES NORTH IN GULF AFTER LASHING TAMPA SECTION

Widespread Damage But No Life Loss Reported On West Coast

The Weather

Marked Ballots Seized at Two Precincts

FOUR VESSELS STANDING BY LINER ON REEF

Await Calm Before Transferring Passengers

Ahead

WILD ELECTION SWEEPS ASIDE OPPONENTS OF CITY MACHINE

Precinct Officials Are Charged With Fraud; Board Subpoenaed

DEATH LIST ON KEYS REPORTED MORE THAN 100

By the mid-1930s, during the depth of the Depression, Tampa had acquired a widespread reputation as a wild town, with illegal gambling rampant and a corrupt political government in charge. It hit an all-time low on September 3, 1935, during the city's hottest municipal election. The National Guard was called out to keep order. Even so there were charges of stuffed ballot boxes, fraudulent voting of all kinds, stolen ballots, and other skullduggery. All this was taking place on a day when a vicious tropical storm was lambasting the community. The event was a showdown clash between two political factions pitting the incumbent mayor, Robert E. Lee Chancey, against former mayor, D. B. McKay. Many citizens reportedly stayed away from the polls because they feared violence. City police were at "war" against the county sheriff's deputies, but no blood was shed. When the polls closed and the paper ballots were counted, Chancey had been reelected by some 4,200 votes. The storm had dealt a severe blow to the state, with 256 persons killed in Florida. The ugly accounts of the day's events triggered a civic reform; voting machines were adopted, a blue ribbon citizens election board was created, and other steps were taken to clean up the town's reputation in future campaigns. Photograph from the author's collection

One of the federal agencies under the New Deal of President Franklin D. Roosevelt during the Depression of the 1930s was the Civilian Conservation Corps. This gave jobs to young men who were unemployed and provided work forces to develop and improve parks and forests in the country. Tampa had a unit of the CCC; it was Company No. 1418, and this was a scene at its camp on June 8, 1936. Photograph by Southern Photo and News, from the author's collection

From 1902 until the 1950s, political rallies were held at Alderman's Ford, just off State Road 39 about ten miles south of State Road 60. After that, politickin' took place more on radio and television and voters did not turn out for live rallies. The ford across the Alafia River was named for James Alderman, pioneer Hillsborough County settler. The pioneer families held picnics at Alderman's Ford before the rallies started, back as early as 1894. This photograph was taken at a political rally at another popular site in the county—Sulphur Springs—in 1936. Among those in the picture who have been identified are Thomas E. Jackson, D. B. Givens, Charles McKay, George H. Wilder, Isaac Brandon, Sim E. Sparkman, Will C. Spencer, D. B. Mc Kay, John G. Robles, B. L. Blackburn, Henry Kruse, Phil Bourquardez, Mrs. Sydney Gibbons, Herbert S. Phillips, Mrs. J. D. Clarke, Mrs. Judge Hanson, Mrs. D. B. Givens, Mrs. Uz Pemberton, and Bill Block. Photograph from the author's collection

Criminals called him "Judge Put-'Em-Away." Judge W. Raleigh Petteway was a tough, no-nonsense, law-and-order jurist, but a very popular citizen and public official in Tampa. He served as Judge of Juvenile Court and later as Judge of the Criminal Court. A pillar of the First Baptist Church, he was an outstanding Sunday school teacher for many years. In 1936, Judge Petteway was a candidate for governor of Florida—and he made an impressive run for it. That was the year the state had a bumper crop of Democratic candidates—fourteen in all. The Tampan was high man in the first primary, with a total of 51,705 votes. This photograph was made on the night of the first primary and the judge was a happy man. Petteway went into the runoff with Lake City's Fred P. Cone, who had collected but 46,842 votes in the first. Cone was a banker and legislator and had served as president of the state senate in 1911. In the runoff, Cone bested Petteway, 184,540 to 129,150. Photograph by Gerald B. Smith of the Tampa Daily Times, *from the author's collection*

William G. Brorein, president and founder of the Peninsular Telephone Company, was a beloved citizen of Tampa. He came here from his native Ohio in 1901 and started the firm from scratch with a subscribers' list of 350. Southern Bell was operating here at the time. There wasn't enough business for one company, let alone two. Eventually, Brorein bought out Bell—the only instance of a local independent buying out the nationwide Bell System. Brorein was active in everything—president of the Florida State Fair and Gasparilla Association, the Rotary Club, Board of Trade (Chamber of Commerce), the YMCA, the Knights of Pythias, the First Christian Church, and a myriad of other organizations. The photo shows Brorein placing the cornerstone on the company's headquarters bulding in Tampa in October 1936, commemorating the thirty-fifth anniversary of the founding of the firm. Brorein died December 12, 1937 at the age of seventy-six. He was succeeded to presidency of the company by his faithful nephew, Carl D. Brorein, who also was for many years a prominent civic leader. Peninsular Telephone Company finally sold out to General Telephone Company, which now serves the community. Photograph from the author's collection

One of the favorite hangouts for young people in the 1930s was the Big Orange drive-in on Lafayette Street (now Kennedy Boulevard) at the railroad track near Willow. The carhops were the prettiest in town, and, of course, this was a lively spot. This picture was snapped August 1, 1936. Ferman Oldsmobile now is situated on this spot. Photograph by Robertson-Fresh, from the author's collection

Florida academicians huddle on the stage of McKay Auditorium to bestow an honorary degree from the University of Tampa upon Governor David Sholtz (back to camera) on June 9, 1936. At left is University of Tampa Dean Morris S. Hale and at right is Dr. John J. Tigert, president of the University of Florida. Photograph by the Tampa Daily Times, *from the author's collection*

The scene here is a busy business neighborhood in the 5000 and 5100 blocks of Florida Avenue in Seminole Heights in 1936. At the extreme left is Riley's grocery, then came the Seminole Theater, Schuler's Sinclair Service, and the popular Seminole Sandwich Shop. Photograph from the author's collection

Yes, we do have bananas—by the bunch and by the boatloads. The delicious fruit is brought here from Central America and unloaded at the banana docks on Thirteenth Street. This picture was made in the 1930s, but the same scene is repeated today. Photograph by Burgert Brothers, from the author's collection

For many years the Dixie Tennis Tournament drew top net stars to Tampa. It was played on the Davis Islands courts and was both a sports and social event. Here is seen some of the action during the 1940 Dixie competition, along with a good view of the Davis Islands Tennis Clubhouse. Photograph from the author's collection

Don Budge played here during the Dixie Tennis Tournament. So did scores of other tennis greats. A perennial winner was Bitsy Grant, the Atlanta businessman and pro tennis player. Bitsy is shown receiving his trophies from Nash Higgins, Superintendent of Public Recreation in Tampa, after winning the singles title in the 1937 tournament. Higgins also was athletic director and head coach of the University of Tampa and at one time was a coach at the University of Florida. Photograph from the author's collection

One of the newspaper greats of Florida of all time was Edwin Dart Lambright, widely quoted editor of the Tampa Tribune *for decades. A native Georgian, he moved to Tampa on June 1, 1899, starting on the* Tribune *as city editor. He was continuously on the paper, with the exception of six years (1917-1923) when he served as Postmaster of Tampa, until his death in 1959. Photograph from the author's collection*

Two personalities usually seen around the Tampa Terrace Hotel in the late 1930s were Max Plattner, left, who directed the orchestra there, and L. Spencer Mitchell, long-time general manager of radio station WDAE, which had its studios on the top floor of the Terrace. Photograph from the author's collection

George H. Mason, owner of the Tampa Terrace Hotel and the Floridian Hotel, left, sips beer as he visits with his pal, Sol Fleischman, popular announcer of radio station WDAE in 1936. Photograph from the author's collection

The First Baptist Church of Tampa has always had an outstanding music program. Conrad Murphree was the director when this photo was made on December 10, 1938. The pastor of the church, Dr. Adiel J. Moncrief, is shown seated in front of the choir. Today, Dr. Moncrief is retired but still serves as a religion writer for the Tampa Tribune-Times. *Photograph by Robertson-Fresh, from the author's collection*

For three quarters of a century or more, a delightful downtown rendezvous was Tibbett's Corner at the corner of Franklin Street and Lafayette Street (now Kennedy Boulevard). Generations of Tampans ate here; although the food was not elegant, the atmosphere was pleasant. This photo was made in April 1938. An advertisement for Old Union Beer is seen underneath the sidewalk canopy. The little booth at the corner was the control booth for the streetcar system operated by Tampa Electric Company for so many years. Incidentally, streetcar tracks crossed at this intersection, and there were usually transfers made here. Note the hanging traffic light with no left turns permitted. The Coca Cola truck was on site delivering crates of drinks to Tibbett's. The skyscraper in the background was the Bay View Hotel. This whole area was razed in the late 1970s to make way for the new Tampa Center. Photograph by Robertson-Fresh, from the author's collection

The Office, Larry Ford's emporium, at 610-12 Tampa Street, was a popular watering hole for downtown businessmen in the 1930s. Beside pretty hostesses, The Office featured cartoons of local celebrities on the wall. Seen here are sketches of O. W. (Doc) Kuhn, Dr. Dan Galvin, J. C. O'Neal, Otto Pelham, Leon Weisberg, W. M. (Jack) Miles, and Farley Price. Photograph by Robertson-Fresh, from the author's collection

The handsome Plant High School had been opened less than a decade when this informal shot was made in the late 1930s. The school was named in honor of Henry Bradley Plant, who brought the railroad to Tampa in the 1880s and opened the elegant Tampa Bay Hotel in 1891. Photograph from the author's collection

For many years, Tampa Electric Company had its corporate offices and retail salesroom in a building at Tampa and Cass streets. In those days, TECO was encouraging the use of electricity for cooking and other household services. It carried a full line of appliances and sold direct to the public. One of the promotions Advertising Director Jack Lacey came up with was a series of newspaper advertisements of prominent Tampans photographed in their electrically equipped kitchens preparing their favorite dishes. These guys were members of the Ancient and Honorable Order of Coqui. One of the Coquis was Dennis B. Rawls, Sr., shown here in his kitchen in his new home at 2202 Azeele Street in July 1939, preparing his specialty, fried shrimp. Rawls himself was an institution in the city. A native of Alabama, he came to Tampa in 1914 and the following year entered the undertaking business. For many years he was manager of B. Marion Reed Funeral Home. He died in 1956. Photograpy by Robertson-Fresh, from the author's collection

Baseball's great Bambino, the incomparable Babe Ruth, once wrote Manuel Rubin, who operated Rubin's Spanish Restaurant at 1403 Tampa Street: "For 17 years I have enjoyed your food and will come back for 17 more, because it is so good." Rubin's was the gathering place for celebrities and for the not-so-great. The superb food and the romantic Latin atmosphere attracted baseball writers and players; film stars Frances Langford and Jon Hall; cartoonist Frank Willard, creator of Moon Mullins; and Chick Young, creator of Dagwood; and thousands of others. Why, it was here at Rubin's that Chick Young—watching the Rubin's chef put together a massive Cuban sandwich—conceived the idea of the Dagwood Sandwich, featured in the cartoon many, many times. A 1939 menu at Rubin's featured a Spanish regular dinner for $1.50, offering bean soup, Pompano al Papillo, baked in paper, vegetable salad, chicken or filet steak, and cream cheese with Cuban preserves and coffee. A two-dollar "Special Spanish Dinner" was an even greater bargain. Rubin's closed in 1957. Photograph by Robertson-Fresh, from the author's collection

Let's drop in the newly air-conditioned Morrison's Cafeteria at 608 Florida Avenue to enjoy the delicious (and cheap!) specials for breakfast, lunch, or supper, on a day in July 1937. If we can scrape up another nickel, we can get a banana and pecan salad with whipped cream! Photograph of Tampa Morning Tribune *ad from the author's collection*

Champion Florida cattle strut by the grandstand at the Florida State Fair in the late 1930s. Photograph from the author's collection

The Rubin brothers, Manuel, (left) and Jose, are squeezed by one of their favorite customers at Rubin's Spanish Restaurant one night in 1938—the big, bruisin' world heavyweight champion boxer, Jack Dempsey. Photograph from the author's collection

One of the most delightful pastimes in town was dancing under the stars at the patio of the Cuban Club. Such was the occasion when this interesting photograph was made on the evening of October 15, 1939. Photograph by Robertson-Fresh, from the author's collection

Pioneer aviator Clarence Chamberlin was inched out in history by Charles Lindbergh, but he made big news just the same. Two weeks after Lindy's historic nonstop flight across the Atlantic in 1927, Chamberlin carried the first passenger across the ocean and wound up landing on a farm in Eisleben, Germany. He and his partner in the venture, New York businessman Charles A. Levine, were dubbed Heroes Two and Three and received a world of publicity for their feat. Their journey of 3,905 miles topped Lindbergh's 3,610. In the years immediately following his famed flight, Chamberlin formed a flying circus and barnstormed around the country. He was described as "one of the last of the nation's propeller-cranking, hell-for-leather pilots who flew by the seat of their pants, the daring of their guts, the love of their women—and their faith in a many-splendored future." In the spring of 1937, Chamberlin showed up in Tallahassee with a couple of World War I Martin bombers converted into passenger planes. He tried to get the legislature that year to give him a charter to operate an intrastate airline. He flew the politicians—including State Senator Spessard L. Holland (later governor and U.S. senator), a World War I aviator—and lobbied them in the process. But he failed to get the charter. He's shown here in 1938 visiting Tampa's Mayor R. E. L. Chancey (holding glasses). Photograph by the Tampa Daily Times, *from the author's collection*

During the late 1930s and early 1940s, the Ku Klux Klan movement enjoyed a revival in Florida and in the Tampa area. This photo, taken at an undisclosed location, shows a large gathering of Tampans brought together to welcome the Imperial Wizard of the Klan, Dr. James A. Colescott. An electrically lighted cross burned brightly on front of the the stage. In 1941, Colescott told a closed session of the House Committee on Un-American Activities in Washington that Florida had more Klan members than any other state. In 1951, the Florida Legislature made it illegal to go masked in public streets or burn crosses in any public place. The law was passed at the urging of Governor Fuller Warren, who flailed out at the Klan as a bunch of "covered cowards, hooded hoodlums, sheeted jerks"—at the same time disclosing he once joined the KKK when that was the thing to be done by aspiring politicians (he being one). Photograph by Robertson-Fresh, from the author's collection

Call it what you will, jitterbugging was the dance craze in 1939 when this action photo was taken at a University of Tampa hop. The students were having a great time in the Dome Room of the old Tampa Bay Hotel, where multimillionaires played and danced in the early part of the century. Photograph from the author's collection

WAR

EXTRA TAMPA MORNING TRIBUNE EXTRA

46TH YEAR—No. 244 | Entered as Second Class Matter Postoffice Tampa, Florida | TAMPA, FLORIDA, FRIDAY, SEPTEMBER 1, 1939 | PRICE FIVE CENTS

HITLER ATTACKS POLES

Hitler Says He Will Win Back Polish Corridor

Tells Reichstag He Will Achieve Return of Danzig or Die Fighting; Names Goering Successor If He Is Killed.

BERLIN, Sept. 1.—(Associated Press.)—Adolf Hitler declared to the German nation today he would achieve the return of Danzig and Pomorze (Polish corridor) and halt Polish attacks on Germans or die fighting.

Hitler told a momentous gathering of the Reichstag today that Field Marshal Goering would be his successor if he should meet death in war.

The fuehrer said that German arms are the most efficient in the world, following this declaration with the disclosure of Goering as his first choice to succeed him and his deputy, Rudolf Hess, as his second choice.

Hitler plunged directly into the subject of Poland and Danzig by declaring:

"We meet to solve the problems raised by the Versailles treaty."

"Force With Force"

Denying the Reich is not peaceably inclined—the fuehrer less than five hours before had announced his army was meeting "force with force" because of alleged border violations by the Poles—declared that we "tried to solve many problems peacefully."

"Fifteen years of peaceful effort to meet this issue were of no avail," he added.

"Danzig is German. The corridor (Pomorze) was and is German.

"More than 1,000,000 Germans who lived in this territory had to leave their homes in 1919 and 1920.

"The dictate of Versailles is not a law for us Germans," he declared in a strong voice.

Reciting Germany's peaceful efforts, he said Germany had made proposals for revision of "unbearable conditions" in Austria, the Sudetenland of Czecho-Slovakia and other places but all without result.

"We also proposed a solution of the corridor problem. It was clear that it had to be solved," he shouted as the Reichstag cheered.

Hitler said he had spoken frequently with Polish statesmen about the corridor problem and finally drew up a moderate formula for meeting the issue.

Great Applause

"Only I could make such terms," he said to great applause.

"These proposals were rejected. The answer (by Poland) was first mobilization and then pressure on Danzig."

Hitler said Germany always had treated fairly the Polish minority in Germany. Then related that the Polish ambassador was called and informed that Germany no longer would look on quietly if "abuse" of German minorities in Poland and ultimatums to Danzig continued.

"I have left no doubt that the Germany of today nowise resembles the Germany of the Hohenzollerns.

"No great power would long tolerate such conditions. I made a last attempt by proposing to Britain that she play the role of mediator.

"I sought to establish a direct connection between Germany and Poland."

This apparently was a reference to the moderate 16-point settlement proposal upon which Germany had expected Warsaw to send a negotiator to Berlin.

"I sat for two days with my government waiting for a Polish plenipotentiary without seeing him," the fuehrer said.

Loves Peace

Hitler declared his love of peace and patience was worn out and so he had informed the British government last night that negotiations were broken off.

To great applause Hitler said he had decided to "talk as Poland talks"—with force.

He denied that western powers have any legitimate interest in the Polish corridor or Danzig.

"We want nothing from the western powers and we have formally declared we have no claims against them. Our west wall (of fortifications) is also our west border."

Hitler referred to the non-aggression pact with Soviet Russia, saying that Germany did not propose to export the Nazi doctrine and saw no reason for further separation from Russia.

"I do not want to wage a battle on women and children," Hitler declared, but he added that if the "enemy" dared to wage "another" war of that sort he would answer "bomb for bomb and gas for gas."

(A transcript of Hitler's speech as taken down in London showed that at this point he thanked Italy for support and said: "I will not appeal to foreign help in this fateful hour. We will carry out this task ourselves.")

CHAMBERLAIN CALLS CABINET TO CONSIDER NAZI ATTACK

Parliament Called To Meet in Special Session This Afternoon

By WEBB MILLER
United Press Staff Correspondent

LONDON, Sept. 1.—(United Press.)—Prime Minister Chamberlain called the cabinet into emergency session today and parliament was called to meet this afternoon.

Albert Forster's decree announcing Danzig's union with Germany, Adolf Hitler's response that a law effecting the reunion would be effected immediately, and Polish announcements of the bombing of Warsaw and other towns, had come as a complete and horrifying surprise.

Polish Note Expected

In view of the Polish announcement that fighting was actually in progress, it was expected that the next diplomatic step would be a Polish note to Great Britain and France invoking their military aid under their alliances, which provide that if Poland considered her independence menaced and resists, Britain and France will go to her aid.

Prime Minister Chamberlain had already announced that if the test came Britain would resist force with force and to the uttermost.

People Flee London

This warm and sunny day found the first contingment of 3,000,000 children, mothers, expectant mothers, blind people and cripples starting to leave London and all key industrial and port and naval towns. Nine main arteries leading out of London had been made one-way outward streets for evacuation by road of others who desired to seek safety from air bombs.

But the dramatic news from Berlin and Warsaw found Londoners, oblivious, going cheerfully to work.

Caught Unaware

The government itself had been caught unaware by Germany's 16 demands on Poland last night.

Morning newspapers had published nothing of the Forster-Hitler proclamations, or the Warsaw charges of German bombings and frontier attacks.

United Press staff observers at one great railroad station saw but one girl, among thousands of people coming in to work, carrying a gas mask.

Read To Ambassador

The German 16 points, which formed the basis for German action, on the ground that Poland had failed to send a plenipotentiary to negotiate on them, were read hurriedly last night to Sir Nevile Henderson, ambassador to Germany, at the Berlin foreign office, a reliable informant said.

Henderson was then told that inasmuch as it was already too late to do anything about it they were not being handed to him officially.

The ambassador was told that on Tuesday the German government had requested that a Polish negotiator arrive in Berlin by Wednesday midnight and that inasmuch as he had not arrived, the German proposals

(Continued on Page 8—Column 4)

Hitler Reichstag Speech Summary

BERLIN, Sept. 1. — (Associated Press. — A summary of the translation of Adolf Hitler's speech to the Reichstag today follows:

"We have all been suffering under the torture which the treaty of Versailles has brought us.

"Danzig was and is a German city.

"Minorities in the Polish corridor have been shamefully mistreated.

"As always I have tried to solve the problem by peaceful means.

"For 15 years there have been opportunities to bring about these revisions but nothing has been done.

"All the proposals to remedy these unbearable conditions did not receive any consideration.

"You know the proposals that I have made to bring about the return of German territories.

"Therefore it is understandable that action must be taken by us.

Tried Peaceful Means

"I have tried by peaceful means to bring about a solution of the Danzig and corridor problems.

"This problem would eventually be solved, but the time it would take would not be satisfactory and has not been satisfactory to us.

"At last I have formulated the German proposals and I must say that they are very modest.

"These proposals that I have made were declined and instead they were answered by mobilizations and by heavy reprisals against the German populations in those areas.

"I have warned, time and time again, and over three weeks ago warned the English that the existing conditions in Danzig could not continue. One must be careful not to mistake the present day Germany with the former Germany.

"Provocations have occurred and no great power can stand by and see these provocations continue.

"I have tried to accept the British proposal, but Great Britain wanted us to take up this question directly with Poland.

Waited Two Days

"I carefully worked out these proposals and have been sitting here for two days waiting to hear from Poland.

"If one expects the German Reich and the German head of the state to accept these conditions then there is nothing else for them to do but to retire.

"In answer to my last proposal a general mobilization was ordered in Poland.

"I have therefore decided to speak to the Poles in the same language as they are speaking to us."

Berliners Warned Against Air Raids

BERLIN, Sept. 1.—(U.P.)—Notices mobilizing downtown civil air defense members appeared in the windows of downtown restaurants and shops about 9 a. m.

In some districts of Berlin, air raid wardens banged on apartment doors about 7 a. m., warning the occupants to be ready for air raid precautions.

FIGHTING ALL ALONG BORDER

BERNE, Switzerland, Sept. 1.—(A.P.)—The Neue Zurcher Zeitung's correspondent in Berlin wrote today:

"It is declared here categorically that the fuehrer's proclamation amounts to opening a state of war. Military operations were begun at 6 a. m. along the entire German-Polish frontier."

'It's Started,' Says Daladier

PARIS, Sept. 1. — (U.P.)—Premier Daladier, entering Elysee palace for a meeting of the council of minsters today, said: "It's started."

"We've done everything we could to avoid it," he added.

Artillery Fire Heard on Border

GLEIWITZ, Germany, Sept. 1.—(A.P.) — (Direct.) — Gleiwitz residents reported artillery fire was heard "in the distance" at 5:30 a. m. today (11:30 p. m., E.S.T., Thursday). Gleiwitz is but a few miles from the Polish Silesian border."

War Summary

Hitler says he will win back Danzig and corridor or die fighting.—Page 1.
Roosevelt informs army and navy of Nazi hostilities.—Page 1.
Roosevelt gets word of Nazi attack on Poland.—Page 1.
Chamberlain calls cabinet to meet; parliament may follow.—Page 1.
Britain moving 500,000 children from London.—Page 8.
French cabinet called.—Page 8.
Danzig reunion with Germany proclaimed.—Page 8.

ROOSEVELT GETS WORD OF NAZI ATTACK ON POLAND

Told 4 Polish Cities Are Bombed; Expected To Summon Congress

BULLETIN

WASHINGTON, Sept. 1. — (A.P.) — President Roosevelt today asked all potential participants in a European war to pledge themselves against bombarding civilian populations or unfortified cities from the air.

The chief executive's appeal was sent at 4:30 a. m. (E.S.T.) to the governments of Great Britain, France, Italy, Germany and Poland.

He requested "an immediate reply."

WASHINGTON, Sept. 1.—(Friday.) (United Press.) — President Roosevelt announced early today that he had received official word that Germany has invaded Poland.

A White House spokesman said the President was advised officially at 2:50 a. m. of the German invasion by

(Continued on Page 8—Column 5)

Ambulance Brings Wounded Soldiers To Nazi Hospital

GLEIWITZ, Germany, Sept. 1. — (A.P.)—An army ambulance carrying wounded soldiers arrived at the emergency hospital here today at 9:10 a. m. (3:10 a. m., E. S. T.).

The men, carried in a wagon, were on stretchers. One had a first aid field bandage. It could not be ascertained where the ambulance came from.

At about 9:30 a half-mile long truck train manned by the engineering corps drove though the heart of the city with pontoon bridge building material. In the train were caterpillar tread, 20-passenger motor vans.

Obviously the train had been on the road for a considerable time. All equipment was thickly covered with gray mud.

A scouting plane of the air force was patroling an area over Gleiwitz.

Early today Gleiwitz residents reported artillery fire was heard "in the distance" a few miles from the Polish-Silesian border.

A number of war dispatches from Europe, in this extra edition of The Tribune, were received last night and this morning before Hitler issued his proclamation, with resulting hostilities. Some may seem strange in view of later developments.

Nazi Planes Bomb Warsaw; Army Attacks

Polish Cities Shelled From Air; German Troops Cross Frontier at Several Points; General Fighting All Along Line.

WARSAW, Sept. 1.—(United Press.)—German airplanes bombed the Polish capital at 9 a. m., (4 a. m. EDT) today, it was announced officially, within an hour after German bombardments had been reported in five other cities in Poland.

The bombardment at Warsaw began with heavy detonations outside the city. Apparently most of them were anti-aircraft barrages but some possibly were bombs.

The explosions were almost continuous. Then the drone of big planes was heard.

Terrific Explosion

In another moment there was a terrific explosion near the central station. Anti-aircraft guns were blasting the sky and clouds were visibly breaking up.

The anti-aircraft gunners obviously could not see the planes when they began the constant fire.

People stood immobile in doorways, looking at the sky. The first discernible movement was a flight of pigeons from the roofs. They quickly settled back, then fluttered away again.

At 9:40 a. m., the air raid sirens signaled "all clear." People immediately emerged from cellars and trench shelters and proceeded calmly to work. Buses were on the streets in a few minutes, making their regular runs.

Many Killed

The Exchange Telegraph of Warsaw reported that many were killed and injured in an aerial bombing which destroyed the station and other buildings in the frontier town of Tozew at 6 a. m.

The foreign office immediately charged Germany with aggression, announcing:

"Shortly after 7 a. m., Germans started military action at different points on the frontier. This undoubtedly is German aggression against Poland. Military action now is developing."

The foreign office did not name the places of action.

Bomb Polish Cities

It was reported that the German bombing squadrons had not been large. The government announced that they had bombed among other places, the railway station at Czew, the town of Rypnic and the town of Putzk, near Czew.

Military circles said that "apparently general fighting has begun at most parts of the frontier."

The Polish island, Westerplatte, in Danzig harbor, which has a munitions dump, was reported sending signals indicating that it was being attacked, but the report was not confirmed.

Other reports that Cracow and Katovitz had been bombed were denied in reliable quarters.

Private sources here said heavy fighting was under way at Chojnice, on the northwestern border.

All Men Under Arms

Every able-bodied man in Poland between the ages of 18 and 40 was under arms. Poland has an army of 4,000,000, and although it had less armaments than Germany, it had more men in the field and there were plenty of rifles and bullets for all. Moreover, Polish morale has never been so high and there were millions more men beyond 40, capable and willing to fight.

The army was almost fully mobilized and spread out along the full length of the German and Slovak borders; cities were streaked with newly-dug air raid trench shelters; Gydinia harbor at the mouth of the gulf of Danzig was mined, and, to the limit of its ability, the country was ready to withstand any onslaught of the German war machine.

The foreign office refused all comment. But semi-officially, and typical of comment in the streets, the government radio

(Continued on Page 8—Column 1)

ampans were shocked on the morn-ng of September 1, 1939 when they picked up their Tampa Morning Tribune *and saw the headline WAR n six-inch boxcar letters. Hitler had nvaded Poland in the wee hours of Tampa time and the newspaper put out an EXTRA to tell the folks about t. Life was never the same after that fateful day. Photograph of* Tampa Morning Tribune, *from the author's collection*

Two star reporters for the Tampa Tribune *in the late 1930s were J. A. "Jock" Murray, left, and William B. "Bill" Abbott, Jr., seen here at Peter O. Knight Airport waiting to interview a visiting celebrity. Both were probing, digging reporters and skilled writers. Their copy sang and took the reader right to the scene of the action, with colorful descriptions of the people and events. They covered all the top stories in Florida for several decades. Bill died in 1973. Jock has been retired for a number of years. He is ninety-five years old. Photograph by the author*

Many months before Pearl Harbor, the Tampa Shipbuilding and Engineering Company began turning out ships for the government. The firm received a contract early on for four 10,000-ton steel ships to cost $2 million each. The first one constructed was the Sea Witch, *shown here on launching day. The company later reorganized as the Tampa Shipbuilding Company, Inc., with George B. Howell as president. Another shipbuilding firm, McCloskey and Company, was established in Tampa and turned out 5,000-ton concrete ships. A third yard also was built, the Tampa Marine Corporation, which produced large seagoing tugs. The* Sea Witch *was at Manila when the Japanese bombed that port early in the war, but the captain raced to sea and the ship escaped unharmed. Photograph from the author's collection*

Tampans were mightly proud of their new airport and administration building on Davis Islands, built as a Works Projects Administration (WPA) project in the late 1930s. It was named in honor of Colonel Peter O. Knight, pioneer citizen, prominent attorney, and president of Tampa Electric Company. The terminal was only a twenty-five-cent cab ride and five minutes from downtown. Here's an Eastern Air Lines plane ready to taxi out on March 30, 1939. Photograph by Burgert Brothers, from the author's collection

They also served who stayed at home and built ships. A brawny shipyard worker swings a heavy hammer in this action shot made August 1, 1939 at the Tampa Shipbuilding and Engineering Company. Employment reached a peak of 16,000 and nearly 100 ships were constructed, mostly for the navy. Photograph from the author's collection

Nineteen Thirty-Nine wasn't the best of all years to be graduating from college, what with a deep economic depression still on, high unemployment, and a worldwide war getting underway. But this class of '39 at the University of Tampa appeared happy to get their diplomas, come what may. Photograph by Robertson-Fresh, from the author's collection

One of the attractive landmarks in the heart of downtown was for decades the elegant red brick building of Elks Lodge No. 708 at the southeast corner of Florida Avenue and Madison Street. The structure was erected in 1913 on the site of the homestead of pioneer Tampa leader, Dr. John P. Wall. In the 1950s the Elks brothers decided to sell the property and they moved to a nightclub that had been closed, the Crystal Ball, on Bayshore Boulevard. The Elks' hall downtown was just across the street from the old Hillsborough County Court House and most of the politicians belonged to the club. It was the gathering place for lunch and for evening affairs. Rocking chairs on the verandahs provided ideal resting spots for Elks and their guests. Photograph from the author's collection

The coffee shop at the Columbia Restaurant has been the unofficial political headquarters for three quarters of a century. This was the scene at noon on November 10, 1939. It's called "Columbia the Gem of Spanish Restaurants" and is located on Seventh Avenue and filling the block between Twenty-first and Twenty-second streets. The establishment was founded by Casimiro Hernandez, who was impressed into Spanish naval service as a Cuban and deserted his warship by jumping overboard and swimming to his home shore in 1898. He operated a little restaurant in Havana until he accumulated enough savings to come to the United States in 1904. Almost immediately he opened his little bar in Ybor City. It has expanded through the years and today is operated by Cesar Gonzmart, who is married to the former Miss Adela Hernandez, daughter of Casimiro Hernandez, Jr. and granddaughter of the Columbia founder. The couple's sons also are in on the operation of the popular restuarant. Photograph by Robertson-Fresh, from the author's collection

There once was an official post office with the name Rattlesnake, Florida. It was located on the east approach to Gandy Bridge on the shore of old Tampa Bay between St. Petersburg and Tampa. Rattlesnake was named by the late George K. End who was the original canner of the famous diamondback rattlesnake. The late Ross Allen, later at Silver Springs, also canned the delicacy. End's tourist stop attracted many motorists who also patronized the post office with its unique name. Sometime around the end of World War II, George End met his fate that ended his novel business. He was bitten on the left hand by a rattler he was milking for venom. He died eight hours later. End, a native of Wisconsin, was a former free-lance writer who came here in 1931 from Arcadia. Photograph from postcard, from the author's collection

Tampa housewives were offered some tempting bargains at Riley's and Piggly Wiggly in this advertisement in the Tampa Tribune *on September 26, 1939. Photograph of advertisement, from the author's collection*

Probably the most famous personage to come from the Tampa Bay area in this century is the gifted singer and actress Frances Langford. She grew up in Lakeland and attended Florida Southern College. She aspired to be an operatic singer, but a risky operation in 1930 when she was fourteen years old changed the direction of her career. She started out with a coloratura soprano voice, but when she had her tonsils out she sang a different pitch. She became a pop singer and zoomed to stardom. The Tampa cigar manufacturer, Eli Witt, heard about her from Frank Grasso, well-known local band leader and music teacher. He put Frances on local radio stations WDAE and WFLA. Witt was a friend of Rudy Vallee and got him to give Frances an audition. The rest is history. She went on to become a talented movie star as well as network radio and stage singer. During World War II, she traveled to war fronts all over the world with Bob Hope's USO troop and became the pinup for GIs everywhere. This picture was made in September 1939 when Frances and her handsome husband, Jon Hall, visited her uncle and aunt, Mr. and Mrs. Arthur T. Peacock of 3314 Leona Avenue. They later divorced, and Frances married Ralph Evinrude, the outboard motor magnate. They now live at Jensen Beach on the Florida east coast. Photograph by the author

This was the home of the Tampa Yacht and Country Club on August 14, 1939. It later was replaced with modern quarters. Photograph by Robertson-Fresh, from the author's collection

Evangelist Billy Graham launched his worldwide crusade while a Bible college student here in Tampa in the late 1930s. The North Carolina youth was a student at the old Florida Bible Institute at Temple Terrace (now Trinity College at Dunedin). Billy was graduated in the class of 1940, president of his class and editor of the yearbook. Under his picture in the annual it was noted that Graham's personal aim was to be an evangelist. Prophetically, the class valedictorian, Vera Resue, proclaimed in her address, "The Time is ripe for another Luther, Wesley, Moody" Indeed it came to pass in later years that such a one stepped out from that very Bible college class! There were many firsts for Billy here. He regularly preached at the old Tampa Municipal Trailer Park and Tampa Rescue Mission. He was turned down for a job when the Sulphur Springs Baptist Church declined to hire him. He made his first appearance on the air when, scared stiff and mike-frightened, he spoke on radio station WSUN. He got the call to preach while meditating one night on the eighteenth hole of the Temple Terrace Golf Course, which formed the campus of the college. He was ordained a Baptist minister while conducting a revival as a student preacher at rural Peniel Baptist Church near Palatka. Photograph from The Bible School Days of Billy Graham

FLORIDA FAIR
MP

Chapter 5

1940 through 1949

Karl A. Bickel, retired president of the United Press wire service and resident of nearby Sarasota, once called Tampa "a city without a soul."

That was in 1945, at a time when Tampa was celebrating the end of World War II, was looking ahead for post-war development, and was still suffering from a decade and a half of bad politics, gambling, and corruption of many sorts.

But the fact is that the community already had begun a cleanup of its civic mess long before Bickel sounded off. After hitting bottom in 1935, voting machines were adopted, a blue ribbon citizens' election board was appointed to watch the voting process, and a general cleanup of a run-down city was under way. Even so, gangland killings, gambling wars, and political corruption were to continue until the end of the 1940s.

Throughout World War II, let it be clearly recorded, Tampans worked hard and sacrified for the war effort. The city hosted thousands upon thousands of airmen at MacDill Air Force, Drew Field, and Henderson Airfield. Three shipyards turned out vessels for the government. And, of course, Tampa youths were scattered all over the world in the military services.

The area tackled postwar development with gusto. An Economic Planning Committee had hired professional planners and their staffs, who developed numerous postwar projects to handle the influx of people expected to flock here. Drew Field was turned into a modern airport, a one-way street system was inaugurated in downtown Tampa, a housing boom began, a suburbia was underway and even a couple of shopping centers became a novelty. Tampans looked forward at the end of the decade to many peaceful and prosperous years. Shipyard activity wound down, many military installations closed out, but MacDill Air Force Base remained as a permanent and important military installation guarding the underbelly of the Southeastern United States.

(overleaf)

Crowds jam to get into the entrance of the Florida State Fair on opening day, February 10, 1941. The fairgrounds in those days were located on North Boulevard and Cass Street. Note there is a military policeman (MP) in the foreground to keep an eye on airmen stationed in the area. Photograph by Robertson-Fresh, from the author's collection

One of the exhibits at the Florida State Fair in Tampa in 1940 that caught the eye of Governor Fred P. Cone featured home-grown cotton. The chief executive, right, is shown with Carl D. Brorein, Peninsular Telephone Company executive, president of the fair and prominent civic leader. Governor Cone served the state from 1937 to 1941. He was a Lake City banker and had many relatives in Tampa. Photograph from the author's collection

The enterprising seven Lykes Brothers, sons of pioneer Floridian Dr. Howell Tyson Lykes, built a great cattle and shipping empire and dominated the business scene for decades. A rare portrait shows the seven brothers. It was taken in 1940. Standing (from left) are James McKay Lykes, John Wall Lykes, Frederick Eugene Lykes, and Lipscomb Goodwin (Dick) Lykes. Seated are Howell Tyson Lykes, Jr.; Thompson Mayo Lykes; and Joseph Taliaferro Lykes. Dick's picture was skillfully added from another portrait by Tampa photographer Carl W. Blakeslee. The last surviving Lykes brother, Joseph, died in 1967. Photograph courtesy of Dr. James Ingram, from the author's collection

A delightful annual event at Plant High School back before World War II was the coronation of the Court of Pantherilla. This was the scene of the stage on March 28, 1940 when Doyle E. Carlton, Jr., was crowned king and Mildred Woodbery was chosen queen. As time went by the king took his queen for a bride and they lived happily ever after! Carlton, son of former Governor Doyle E. Carlton, Sr., ran for governor himself in 1960 and was in the Democratic primary runoff. He has become an outstanding businessman, state senator, president of the HavaTampa Cigar Company, cattleman, and church and civic leader. Photograph by Robertson-Fresh, from the author's collection

In 1940, Fulgencio Batista had just become president of our neighboring island of Cuba for his first term. And he was the gracious host when Tampa's Latin American Fiesta Queen and her royal party went to Havana on a good-will visit. Shown here in the Presidential Palace (now a "Museum of the Revolution"), Batista, in white suit, talks animatedly with Queen Hortense Vallina, center, and her sister, Rose, while Tampa restaurateur Manuel Rubin listens attentively. The other gentleman in the photo is an unidentified official of the Cuban Tourist Commission. Photograph from the author's collection

This photograph was taken on November 13, 1940 just as MacDill Air Field was beginning to develop. A visiting high-ranking officer and staff officers were on the reviewing stand watching the airmen march by. Standing in front are Brigadier General Clarence L. Tinker, left, base commander who was to become the first American general officer to be killed in combat in World War II, and his chief of staff, Colonel H. H. Young. Photograph by Southern Photo and News, Inc., from the author's collection

Representative Martin Dies (D-Texas), center, was a highly controversial figure when he came to Tampa to address a rally at the Tampa Municipal Auditorium (now McKay Auditorium) on the evening of January 22, 1941. Dies was a dynamic speaker, tall, handsome, and very serious about his job as chairman of the House Committee on Un-American Activities. The committee was created in 1938. The investigations of Nazi activities which he at first planned soon gave way to inquiries into Communist activities; almost immediately the committee's hearings became a source of sensational stories of infiltration of many aspects of American life by subversives. Dies himself claimed to be more effective in detecting Communist subversion than the Federal Bureau of Investigation (FBI). He died in 1972. Photograph by Robertson-Fresh, from the author's collection

Charles Edgar "Pete" Norton, affable sports editor of the Tampa Tribune, *was out soliciting for Spartan Fund, an aid to athletes at the University of Tampa, when this picture was made on January 27, 1941. He's receiving a check from his pal, Crip, who sold the newspaper on the streets at the corner of Lafayette and Franklin streets for many years. Norton succeeded blustery, hard-hitting V. M. "Red" Newton when the latter stepped up to assistant managing editor back before World War II. Both wrote the popular column "The Morning After," which is now written by the astute Tom McEwen. Photograph from the author's collection*

Co-eds at the University of Tampa reverted to childhood and became babes for the Sigma Kappa Nu fraternity in the spring of 1941. The guys adopted the gals as their daughters. Photograph from the author's collection

This pretty Latin senorita adds color, glamor, and music to the annual La Verbena del Tobaco celebration in 1940. The event saluted Tampa's thriving cigar industry. Note tobacco leaves featured in her costume, including the chapeaux. This photo was shot on June 28, 1941. Photograph by Robertson-Fresh, from the author's collection

"Let's go to the fair" suggests pretty Dot Sigman, shown here holding a car plate advertising the event. Miss Sigman was the popular vocalist with the Manuel Sanchez Band, "the red-headed blues singer" as a newspaper reporter described her. Photograph by the Tampa Daily Times, *from the author's collection*

A group in Tampa known as the Gasparilla Motorcycle Club earned national recognition when it was presented the Safety Award of the American Motorcycle Association for the year of 1940. Members of the club posed for this photo on June 15, 1941 on a boat in the Bayshore Marina. Photograph by Southern Photo and News, from the author's collection

The first commanding officer of MacDill Field, now MacDill Air Force Base, was dashing Brigadier General Clarence L. Tinker. He cut a wide swath in Tampa in the short time he was here, not only in military circles but in social and civic areas as well. He was tall, handsome, part Indian, and personable. He sported neat pork chop sideburns long before these became the fad. He's shown here presenting roses to a participant in a public event. Within a week or ten days after Pearl Harbor. Tinker was transferred to the Pacific theater and was commanding officer of the air force in Hawaii. He was killed in combat early in the war. Photograph from the author's collection

Providing transportation for the thousands of airmen stationed at MacDill Air Force Base to downtown Tampa during World War II was this ferrylike boat. It was a familiar sight as it made its way around the bay and up Hillsborough River. The vessel was affectionately named the General Clarence L. Tinker *in honor of the beloved first C.O. of the bustling base. Photograph from the author's collection*

Tampa's new army air base was dedicated as MacDill Field on April 16, 1941, named in honor of Colonel Leslie MacDill of Monmouth, Illinois, who was killed in a plane crash at Washington, D.C., in 1938. The photograph shows Mayor R. E. L. Chancey broadcasting over radio station WDAE, the Tampa Daily Times *station, while flicking ashes from his ever-present cigar. At the right is General Clarence L. Tinker, base commander, crop in right hand, who was to lose his life in combat in the Pacific soon after the start of World War II. The civilian in the white shirt with sunglasses is Sol Fleischman, veteran chief announcer of the station, who a short time later would go on active duty in the U.S. Coast Guard. The civilian seen between Mayor Chancey and General Tinker is A. T. Rollins, long-time Mayor of Port Tampa City and later Tampa City Councilman. And behind him straightening his tie is Ray B. Cralle, Tampa auto dealer and civic leader. The young man to the left of Fleischman was an engineer for WDAE. Photograph by the Tampa Daily Times, from the author's collection*

Civilian institutions in Tampa worked closely with MacDill Air Force Base to help train airmen months before World War II actually started. Here is Class No. 2, Administrative Clerks, graduating from Tampa Business College on July 31, 1941. The school was at Grand Central Avenue and Edison Street. Photograph from the author's collection

There it is, a sign advertising gasoline for nineteen cents a gallon! And that's for real, because that was the going price at the Spur station on Platt Street at Ashley when the photographer dropped by on August 24, 1941. Is this what they mean by "the good old days"? Photograph by Robertson-Fresh, from the author's collection

A well-known road tavern just before World War II was the Star Light Club far out at 10011 Nebraska Avenue. This was the scene the evening of August 31, 1941. The flags were displayed, but only civilians are seen dancing. Photograph by Robertson-Fresh, from the author's collection

Many years ago there was a popular tune that went "I found a million-dollar baby in a five-and-ten cent store!" Here we have a bevy of pretty clerks at the J. J. Newberry five-and-dime in downtown Tampa. Photo taken on September 7, 1941. Photograph by Robertson-Fresh, from the author's collection

From 1913 through 1972, the Gordon Keller School of Nursing turned out graduate, professional nurses. Here is the class of 1941 on the grounds of Tampa Municipal Hospital, now Tampa General. Officials seated in the center of the front row are Dr. William M. Rowlett, hospital chief of staff; Miss Isobel Meighen, director of nursing; and Ernest G. McKay, superintendent of the hospital. GKSN was a three-year, diploma school. It phased out in 1972 and nurses' training was transferred to Hillsborough Community College. Photograph by Robertson-Fresh, from the author's collection

For sheer, down-to-earth sociable fun, nothing beats an old-fashioned weenie roast on a cool autumn evening. Here a group of employees from Duval Jewelry Company relax at such a social on October 16, 1941, just weeks before Pearl Harbor dashed this country into a shooting war. P. J. Jernigan ran the store and believed in entertaining his personnel. Photograph by Robertson-Fresh, from the author's collection

Units in the Armistice Day Parade, November 11, 1941 proved to be a preview of war. In less than a month, Pearl Harbor had triggered a world-wide conflict. Marching down Franklin Street is a platoon of the home guard. Leading the group is M. M. (Jack) Frost, who later went on active duty in the Air Force, and in civilian life was a top executive for Eastern Air Lines. In the second row, left, is Sol Fleischman, the inimitable chief announcer for radio station WDAE, who soon was in the U.S. Coast Guard. The home guard in the rear row, right, is John N. Harrison, Jr., a Tampa printing executive. Photograph by the Camera Center, from the author's collection

The Fresh Up Committee of the Tampa Junior Chamber of Commerce called on Mayor R. E. L. Chancey in 1941 to receive a proclamation recognizing the community cleanup campaign. From left to right are Willie Houlihan, Gert H. W. Schmidt, Sam Davis, and Mayor Chancey. The Jaycees were an active force in Tampa prior to World War II. Photograph from the author's collection

Collection points were set up around the city to receive donations of scrap aluminum for the national defense drive in 1941. Some Tampa housewives even sacrificed their favorite old cooking pots to boost the movement. Photograph from the author's collection

At the very beginning of World War II, just as MacDill Field, later MacDill Air Force Base, was budding out, artist Will Kay Hagerman did a series of etchings from life at the big installation. This scene was sketched December 12, 1941 for Warren-Henderson Realty Company, Inc., one of Tampa's oldest businesses, dating back to 1887. Photograph of etching by Will Kay Hagerman, from the author's collection

One of the first of the Tampa Housing Authority's low-rent housing developments was Riverview Terrace on Florida Avenue. In an effort to clear slums and provide model, low-rent housing areas, the federal government put up ninety percent and the city of Tampa ten percent of the funding. Photograph by Southern Photo and News, from the author's collection

And another victim goes down as Tampa's Tommy Gomez goes up in his climb in the boxing world! Gomez developed those powerful muscles lugging luggage around the Floridan Hotel as a bellhop in his younger days. He was dubbed "The Beltin' Bellhop" by the Tampa Daily Times *sportswriter Woody Thompson. This picture was made in 1941. Tommy went into the service, was wounded, and was decorated with the Purple Heart. He returned to his hometown after World War II and resumed his promising career. He had risen to be the third-ranking heavyweight in the United States when he was defeated by challenger, later world's heavyweight champion, Jersey Joe Walcott. Photograph from the author's collection*

World War II had officially started a few days before, but Tampans were planning their noisiest, gayest New Year's Eve ever on December 31, 1941. The finest night spot in Tampa, the Tampa Terrace Hotel's Palm Room, was requesting formal dress even though the cover charge was but $2.50 per person. That charge included favors, entertainment, and a New Year's breakfast. The Terrace Lounge also was open for celebrating at a more reasonable $1.00 per person cover charge. This advertisement appeared in the Tampa Morning Tribune *on December 31. Photograph of* Tampa Morning Tribune *ad from the author's collection*

Tampa was abuzz with military activity shortly after Pearl Harbor. Here the Special Aircraft Warning Units of Drew Field are in formation for inspection. Lieutenant Colonel Richard Gimbel was commanding officer, with Major Rex W. LeFevre the C.O. for the 503rd Signal Regiment, AW, and Captain H. C. Floyd, the C.O. for the 553rd Signal Battalion, Sep., AW. The picture was taken on February 7, 1942. Photograph from the author's collection

For years, the city of Tampa operated a Tourist Recreation Center in Plant Park at the rear of the University of Tampa. The tourists came from most of the forty-eight states, and even during war time they were here. This picture was taken on March 12, 1942 and shows the well-dressed visitors getting together for a happy time. Photograph by Robertson-Fresh, from the author's collection

Tampa's Municipal Auditorium *resounds with hundreds of voices as Miss Florence Stumpf of the Hillsborough County School System led a massed concert of students from a number of schools on April 1, 1942. A massed orchestra on the stage accompanied the songsters. Note the high school coeds all were wearing bobby socks. Photograph by Robertson-Fresh, from the author's collection*

It's plain to see what's going on here at Maas Brothers—a sale! Not only that, it is a fabric sale at thirty-three cents a yard. The event packed 'em in on March 4, 1942. Photograph by Robertson-Fresh, from the author's collection

When Milady shopped in Tampa in the spring of 1942, what prices would she expect to pay for clothing? Well, at a sale such as "Falk Days" at O. Falk's, she could buy $1.59 slips for 99 cents, nylon hose for $1.69 a pair and shoes at $1.00 per foot! This advertisement appeared in the Tampa Morning Tribune *on May 1, 1942. O. Falk's, an old-line department store, later operated as Falk's, and finally closed its doors. Photograph of* Tampa Morning Tribune *ad, from the author's collection*

J. Rex Farrior was a real campaigner. He served as state attorney from his appointment in 1933 by Governor David Sholtz until the end of his term in 1953. He gained fame early in his career as prosecutor when he successfully prosecuted the Tampa flogging cases in the mid-1930s. Farrior was a good campaigner and was a fine orator when he got fighting mad, as he did often during a hot political fight. His record as a prosecutor was denounced by U.S. Senator Lester Hunt (D-Wyoming), who handled the Kefauver Crime Committee hearings here in 1950. This photo shows Farrior at a rally of his supporters in Ybor City. Farrior is seen at the center of the stage behind a large portrait of then President Franklin D. Roosevelt. At the back of the stage to Farrior's right is J. Frank Umstot, his assistant. E. O. (Henry) Palermo is the man standing at the extreme left of the stage. Farrior, still active, has practiced law here since 1924. He was graduated from the University of Florida and subsequently coached athletics at his alma mater. Photograph by Robertson-Fresh, from the author's collection

Remember Pearl Harbor! *was the ringing title of the lead feature at the Florida Theater on July 14, 1942. The second show on the bill was* The Wife Takes a Flyer, *starring Joan Bennett and Franchot Tone. The Florida, at 710 Franklin Street opposite the Tampa Theatre, boasted that it was "Air Conditioned—Always Cool and Comfortable." The prices of admission also were comfortable: twenty-eight cents for adults and nine cents for children. Photograph by Robertson-Fresh, from the author's collection*

Volunteers for the Florida Defense Force, or the home guards, went into training immediately after Pearl Harbor. Here is a photo of Company B, Fifth Battalion, taken on June 22, 1942. This close-order drill appears to have taken place in front of a Davis Islands hotel. The unit leader was John N. Harrison, Jr. Photograph by Robertson-Fresh, from the author's collection

Civilians and airmen mixed in the friendly atmosphere of Watts Sanderson's Central Terrace Beer Garden at 1312-14 Central Avenue on July 19, 1942. Photograph by Robertson-Fresh, from the author's collection

This was the scene at the Beulah Baptist Institutional Church at 604 Tyler Street on June 23, 1942. The Reverend William M. Davis was pastor. Photograph by Robertson-Fresh, from the author's collection

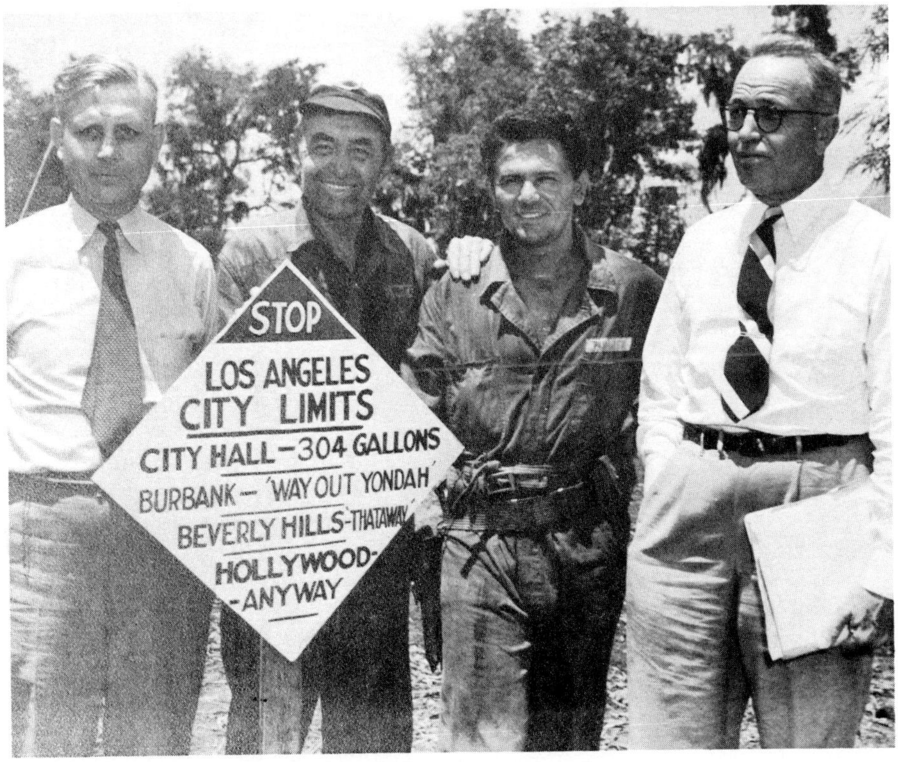

Warner Brothers Pictures came to Tampa early in World War II to film a movie, Air Force, *depicting the aerial war in the Pacific. The movie was shot at Drew Field in August 1942. Shown on the set with a couple of the stars are two officials of the Greater Tampa Chamber of Commerce: T. G. Mixson, president of the chamber, at extreme left, and G. Dave Curtis, secretary of the chamber, extreme right. Photograph from the author's collection*

Before World War II, probably none of these women had even seen a military airplane. But here, on September 10, 1942, this group was learning how to put one together. This was a class in aircraft fabric at Brewster Vocational School with Jack O'Neal as instructor. Photograph by Robertson-Fresh, from the author's collection

This group of handsome women poses on the steps of Centro Asturiano at 1915-17 Nebraska Avenue before holding their meeting in the clubhouse. This picture was taken on November 8, 1942. Photograph by Robertson-Fresh, from the author's collection

The Big Red Terriers of Hillsborough High School rolled through several successful seasons under the tutelage of Head Coach J. Crockett Farnell, and here we see the squad that won the Big Ten Conference championship in 1942. Farnell is standing at right in the rear row. His assistant, Dick Spoto, is at the left end of the same row. Both Farnell and Spoto were stars at the University of Tampa in the 1930s. Farnell later became Hillsborough County school superintendent and Spoto was a high-school principal for many years. Photograph by Robertson-Fresh, from the author's collection

Backing up the 1942 Big Ten Champs at Hillsborough High School was this squad of exhuberant cheerleaders. Left to right: Sis Blanchard, Juanita Black, Tootsie Peerman, Sarah Lee Williams, Elmer Walston, Waldo Lawton, Onie Santana, Marian Mackey, and Esther Kaiser. Photograph from the author's collection

The Tampa Chapter of the American Red Cross was extremely busy during World War II, when it ran training classes to qualify volunteer nurse's aides. Shown is the sixth class trained by Mrs. Norma McMullen, R.N., at graduation. The nurse in center back row is Gertrude Neely. Photograph by Robertson-Fresh, from the author's collection

Another major political contest for mayor of Tampa had ended in September 1943, and official changing of the guard was taking place here. That's outgoing Mayor R. E. L. Chancey on the left and incoming Mayor Curtis Hixon on the right. The man in between is Phil R. Bourquardez, the city clerk, who swore in the new "His Honor." Hixon was a Seminole Heights druggist who had served on the city council and on the county commission. Chancey, a lawyer, had served three terms. Photograph from the author's collection

The Hi-Hat Club in the DeSoto Hotel in downtown Tampa was a popular gathering place for lonesome off-duty airmen. This photo was made October 5, 1942. Lou Figuerdo (civilian standing at left in front) was the operator. An MP (military policeman) is standing behind Figuerdo. Photograph by Robertson-Fresh, from the author's collection

***Jewish soldiers and local friends** observe Passover Seder at the Schaari Zedek Synagogue on April 19, 1943. Photograph by Robertson-Fresh, from the author's collection*

Airmen and soldiers were seen all over town during World War II. Oh yes, and sailors too! This was the scene at Happy's Corner in the 800 block of Florida Avenue between Polk and Cass streets. Photograph from the author's collection

This postcard shows a crash boat in action at MacDill Field (now MacDill AFB) during World War II. The vessel was named the Brigadier General William Mitchell *saluting a controversial air force general of an earlier day. The boats were kept ready to rescue crews from planes which might crash in the many waters around the base. This happened often, so often that there was a saying among the airmen: "A B-26 a day in Tampa Bay!" Photograph by the Army Air Corps, from the author's collection*

These smartly uniformed ushers moved with military precision in escorting customers at the Seminole Theatre. The photo was taken May 25, 1944. Photograph from the author's collection

This window display in F. W. Woolworth's downtown store urged passersby to help win the war by buying War Bonds. The photo was taken on January 21, 1944. Photograph from the author's collection

It's Easter Sunday 1944 and Tampa-based airmen are having a party eating Easter eggs and spinning Frankie Sinatra records at the USO Club on Madison Street. Photograph from the author's collection

Full-dress ceremonies marked the presentation of the coveted Army-Navy E Award to the Tampa Shipbuilding and Engineering Company (TASCO) on July 7, 1944. Photograph from the author's collection

Swing it! The director of the 735th Army Band sets the pace as the military musicians stage a benefit show to promote War Bonds at the Lincoln Theatre on July 7, 1944. Photograph from the author's collection

This quartet of heavyweight Tampa civic leaders were meeting as a Florida Chamber of Commerce committee on December 2, 1944. From left to right are seen: Truman Green, the Tampa Tribune*; Frank M. Traynor, Florida Portland Cement; Carl D. Brorein, Peninsular Telephone Company (now General Telephone Company); and Francis J. Gannon, Tampa Electric Company. Photograph from the author's collection*

As it did throughout the world, the United Service Organization (USO) entertained servicemen on pass or furlough here in Tampa during World War II. The club was at 506 Madison Street and Joe A. Loughrey was the director. This picture shows the young folks enjoying themselves at a dance marking the third anniversary of the USO Club on July 28, 1944. Photograph from the author's collection

Fun-loving sorority sisters at the University of Tampa amused Tampans as they paraded downtown on bicycles—and wearing pajamas. The Delta Kappa event took place in 1945. Note streetcar tracks. Photograph from the author's collection

V-J Day! The war is over! These exuberant Italian-Americans assembled at Eighth Avenue and Eighteenth Street to celebrate V-J Day, the end of World War II, on August 14, 1945. Someone was holding a sign reminding "Remember Pearl Harbor" (upper left hand corner). Photograph courtesy of Tony Pizzo

There were still plenty of airmen and soldiers around Tampa on September 27, 1945, and they were celebrating the end of the war dancing at the Elks' Club. Photograph from the author's collection

For another year, an official of the Cincinnati Reds baseball club signs for use of the facilities of Tampa's Plant Field for their spring training in the late 1940s. Gladly inking the contract for the city are Mayor Curtis Hixon, left, and Recreation Superintendent Nash Higgins, right. Photograph from the author's collection

These World War II veterans, shown returning to the campus of the University of Tampa in 1946, swapped uniforms for mufti. The ex-GIs utilized the GI Bill to finance their education. Photograph from the author's collection

For a while after World War II, Tampa's International Airport operated out of deserted barracks buildings at old Drew Field. This was the scene at the terminal in 1946. That's a National Air Lines plane at the ramp. This limited facility is a far cry from today's magnificent Taj Mahal air terminal at the same airport. Photograph from the author's collection

A massed concert of high school singers was in progress when this photograph was taken April 15, 1947 at Tampa Municipal Auditorium (now McKay Auditorium). Photograph by Robertson-Fresh, from the author's collection

Trolley cars appeared first in Tampa in 1890. From then on they were a vital part of the city's mass transportation system until August 3, 1946, when overnight they were replaced by buses. The streetcars were operated by the Tampa Electric Company. This photograph shows WDAE's Sol Fleischman interviewing the veteran streetcar conductor who piloted the last streetcar on the last run, out to Ballast Point. The staff of the Tampa Daily Times *chartered the trolley for the last run and enjoyed a going away party en route. Photograph by the* Tampa Daily Times *from the author's collection*

Through the years Tampa has produced many splendid barbershop quartets. An oustanding foursome in the 1940s were The Florida Trebles (left to right): Beal H. Siler, Fred Breedon, Sam Breedon, and Richard D. "Dick" Jackson. One must guess who the fifth person is. Photograph courtesy of Richard D. "Dick" Jackson, from the author's collection

In September 1947 Tampa rolled out the red carpet to welcome home its own Mary Hatcher, who had risen to be a top star on stage and screen. She was a graduate of Plant High School. Mary is shown here on the stage of the Tampa Theatre being greeted by Frank Grasso, a superb musician and teacher who had discovered Frances Langford and other stars. He also had a popular dance band which he called the Don Francisco Orchestra and served as musical director of local radio stations. Photograph by Robertson-Fresh, from the author's collection

A modern-day Horatio Alger is James W. Walter. Creator of the Shell Home, he launched his enterprise in 1946 with a pittance, setting up a small office just off Waters Avenue in the Sulphur Springs area. Today he is head of a multimillion-dollar conglomerate with huge headquarters on Dale Mabry Highway. One of his several firms is Celotex Corporation. Photograph from the author's collection

The American flag and the Cuban flag form the backdrop during a meeting of a fraternal group, the Caballeros de la Luz, at the Cuban Club on May 9, 1947. Photograph by Robertson-Fresh, from the author's collection

She holds more aviation and automotive records combined than any other person in history! Only Tampa's Betty Skelton can make this statement. This petite lady (five foot, three and one-half inches tall, ninety-eight pounds, twenty-two-inch waist) has torn up the skies, the raceways, and even the waterways in high-speed boats. She is laden with as many talents as she is titles. Beside all her daredevilry, she is a skilled businesswoman, has a record as a successful advertising executive, has a background in radio and television, and is the holder of many beauty contest honors. Betty Skelton is the first and one of the few woman test drivers in the auto industry. She is the first and only woman three-time winner of the world's stunt flying title . . . the first and only woman to receive an AAA race driver's license . . . the first woman to pilot an Indianapolis race car, a jumpboat, and a Gold Cup racing boat. Betty performed at air shows all over the world. One popular trick was to cut horizontal ribbons with the wing tips of her plane—flying only eight feet above ground. Many Tampans recall when Betty used her plane to pull the cork from the immense liquor bottle on a water tank atop the Knight and Wall building at Tampa and Lafayette streets as an advertising stunt. She's shown here arriving at Honeymoon Isle off Dunedin in 1947. Photograph from the author's collection

Tampa's exquisite Los Novedadas Restaurant at 1430 E. 7th Avenue in Ybor City was a well-lit, popular night spot when this photograph was taken on January 23, 1947. A capsule history: In 1890, when Las Novedadas was founded by its original proprietor, Manuel (Canuto) Menendez, Ybor City was a tiny village barely four years old. Ybor City's pioneer cigarmakers made Los Novedadas their favorite rendezvous and over Cuban coffee and Spanish pastry called "las novedadas" or "the novelties" they would spend their leisure hours discussing the affairs of the day. Gradually the tiny coffee shop became known as Los Novedadas, and in this casual manner the name of Tampa's oldest and one of its finest Spanish restaurants was born. During the Spanish-American War, Teddy Roosevelt's Rough Riders gained local fame when they gayly galloped into the small restaurant, and the Latin inhabitants termed the escapade "The Charge of the Yellow Rice Brigade." Las Novedadas went on to become one of the nation's finest ethnic restaurants, featured and recommended by Holiday, McCalls, Gourmet International, Esquire, Ladies' Home Journal, *the* Saturday Evening Post, *and the American* Automobile Association. *Photograph by Robertson-Fresh, from the author's collection*

Happy Tampans and their guests were enjoying their arroz con pollo *and* potaje de garbanzos *in a main dining room of Las Novedadas Restaurant on a typical evening in January 1947. That's the owner of the restaurant, Manuel Garcia, standing near front at left. The establishment continued in popularity for many more years, but finally in November 1972 it closed its doors as the Las Novedadas. Photograph by Robertson-Fresh, from the author's collection*

Aren't they cute little angels? This was the First Communion class at St. Joseph's School on April 15, 1947. Photograph from the author's collection

Good-looking actor Tyrone Power, with top coat and brief case, is greeted by Dr. E. C. Nance, president of the University of Tampa, upon his arrival at the Tampa International Airport. Standing beside the star is Jean Burnett, Miss Tampa of 1948. Power was in town to give the commencement address to the university's graduating class. A Tampa U. history states that Power gave his speech "in a sincere manner." The movie heartthrob was conferred an honorary degree from the university as he ended his talk. Photograph from the author's collection

Carl J. Sedlmayr, Sr., was a showman and a businessman. He's the man who put together and developed the Royal American Shows, which became the world's largest railroad carnival. It wintered in Tampa for many years and was a feature at the Florida State Fair until 1981. In 1948 a movie was made depicting the life of Sedlmayr called, King of the Carnival. *At the local premiere on March 19, 1948, Sedlmayr (extreme left) was the honored guest, of course. Posing in the photograph taken at the opening are Sally Rand, of Chicago World's Fair fan dance fame, who traveled with Royal American shows a year or two; Carl O. Gabbert, a local friend; and Mayor Curtis Hixon. Sedlmayr's son, C. J. Jr., who literally grew up in the carnival, now heads the vast organization. Photograph from the author's collection*

Presenting: "The Amazing New KAISER." That's what the banner on the wall behind the shiny automobile proudly proclaims. It's the premier showing of a new brand-name vehicle at the Florida State Fair in Tampa on February 4, 1947. The local dealer was Florida Trading Post, Inc. The Kaiser and its sister car the Frazer were advertised as "America's First 1947 Motor Cars." The cars failed to capture the American market and soon became relics of the postwar economy. Photograph by Robertson-Fresh, from the author's collection

On July 11, 1948 the city of Tampa saluted the famed aviatrix on Betty Skelton Day, so proclaimed by Mayor Curtis Hixon. That was the day she tried to set a new international speed record at Peter O. Knight Airport. She nearly lost her life that day when the Rolls-Royce engine in her P-51 blew up, but she expertly brought her crippled craft to a safe dead stick landing at MacDill Air Force Base. When asked why she didn't bail out over Tampa Bay, Betty joked she didn't know how to swim! In 1960, Look *magazine wanted to know if a woman—whose lighter weight would require a rocket with considerably less thrust than that needed for a man—could endure the stresses of space flight. Betty was chosen for the experiment and spent four months being tested, twisted, whirled, and tested again by a small army of doctors and technicians. She endured what the astronauts had endured. She was dubbed Miss Seven and One-Half by the original seven astronauts. Betty is now Mrs. Donald Frankman and operates a real estate firm in Winter Haven. She's shown here in her acrobatic plane, the Pitt Special* Little Stinker. *The plane now rests in the Sports Hall of Fame at Cypress Gardens. Betty attended Plant High and the University of Tampa. Photograph from the author's collection*

Babe Didrikson Zaharias, (center in photo) named by the Associated Press *as the Top Woman Athlete of the Half Century 1900 to 1949, became a permanent resident of Tampa in her later years. In 1937 she married fame wrestler George Zaharias, billed as "The Crying Greek from Cripple Creek." The couple liked Tampa and decided to make it their home. Babe always wanted a golf course of her very own. So, in 1941, George bought the old Forest Hills Golf and Country Club, which was built in 1924 as part of this ritzy real estate development. The clubhouse itself cost $200,000. Babe and George renamed the layout the Tampa Golf and Country Club. The couple first lived on the course, and later built their dream house at 11503 North Rome on Lake Echols. George was forced to sell the club in 1954 for a reported quarter million dollars when the pressures of Babe's illness with cancer made it impossible to care for her and run the course, too. Babe entered a Texas hospital in the spring of 1956 and, after a six-month stay, died on September 27 at the age of forty-three. The course is now owned by the City of Tampa and is called the Babe Zaharias Golf and Country Club. Photograph by the* Tampa Daily Times, *from the author's collection*

The Joie Chitwood Thrill Show is based in Tampa and performs all over North America before fairground audiences as well as on television and in the movies. Joie Citwood, Sr., shown in this 1949 photo ready for another thriller, started it all in 1943 when he acquired the rolling stock from the estate of another great stunt driver, Lucky Teter, who was killed in attempting a ramp-to-ramp jump. Today there are three generations of Joie Chitwoods, all in the thrill show business. Actually, Joie, Sr., has retired but still keeps an eye on the company. His two sons, Joie, Jr., and Tim head up twin troupes that fan out all over the country. And then there's Joie III, who is growing up in the business. Photograph from the author's collection

Joie Chitwood, Sr., at one time a racer in the Indianapolis 500, is seen performing at the Florida State Fair in his home town on February 2, 1949. This was on the track in front of the old Plant Field grandstand. Photograph from the author's collection

The American Legion was formed by veterans of World War I. One of the founders was Tampa's Lieutenant General Sumter L. Lowry. Since the beginning, veterans of later wars have been admitted. The Legion always has been active in Tampa and many of the city's top business and civic leaders have participated in its affairs. The first unit here was the U.S.S. Tampa *Post No. 5. It was named in memory of the U.S.S.* Tampa, *which on September 26, 1918, was sunk in the English Channel while escorting submarines into dangerous waters. All 191 hands on board were lost, including twenty-five Tampa men. This photograph shows some of the top Legionnaires in the city as they gathered on March 29, 1949. Front row, left to right: Colonel H. C. Culbreath, second man unidentified, J. C. Huskisson, Pat Reece, William J. Placie, Chester Kurtz, Gettis B. Henderson, William B. Hopkins, and Howard P. Macfarlane. Rear row: Morris E. White, Guy Allen, Judge William C. Brooker, James C. Handly, T. Paine Kelly, Henry H. Cole, Frank Willis, William Earl Thompson, Colonel Max J. Mackler, Judge L. A. Grayson, M. L. "Monty" Montgomery, Heiskell Harvill, Curtis Sparkman, and Peyton T. Jordan, Sr. Photograph by Robertson-Fresh, from the author's collection*

Back before the advent of television in the Tampa area, political rallies used to attract thousands of persons. The biggest ones were held in the band shell at Plant Park or at the courthouse square downtown. One of the best orators and most popular candidates to hit the town was Fuller Warren, the "barefoot boy from Blountstown," who became governor in January 1949. Warren is shown here speaking at a rally late in the campaign on the night of May 13, 1948. He set up his platform on the sidewalk beside Resnick's Restaurant facing toward the courthouse square, and thousands of his followers jammed into the area. Madison Street had been closed off between Franklin Street and Florida Avenue. Warren was strong in Hillsborough County and carried it over Dan McCarty by a vote of 24,306, to 19,722 in the runoff. McCarty was heavily boosted by the Tampa Morning Tribune, *which ran front page cartoons by George White and numerous editorials favoring the Fort Pierce candidate. Photograph from the author's collection*

John H. Dolcater was a genial, fun-loving, successful Tampa businessman who liked to host parties at his lumber company. In several of the organizations in which he was active the usual top event of the year was when the group was invited for oysters and fish fries. Dolcater is seen here at the head of the chow line leading his guests to the serving table. The ladies' auxiliaries were assisting in the serving, all wearing funny hats to add to the gaiety of the affair. Dolcater was active in the Greater Tampa Chamber of Commerce, the Rotary Club of Tampa, and numerous other organizations. Photograph from the author's collection

All dressed up and wearing their best smiles, these children in Mrs. Bertha F. Hood's fourth grade posed prettily for the photographer who visited Henry Mitchell School in 1949. These boys and girls are now reaching middle age and most of them probably have children, and perhaps grandchildren. The school was named for Governor Henry L. Mitchell, one of two Tampans to be elected governor of Florida. Photograph by Robertson-Fresh, from the author's collection

Tampa businessman Tom Spicola was owner of the Tampa Smokers professional baseball club for a number of years after World War II. As seen in this photograph, Spicola made a walking advertisement for his team because he always had a Tampa-made cigar in his mouth. The sports enthusiast was an official of the family-owned Spicola Hardware Company. Photograph by Henry Rod, from the author's collection

Publicists for the Greater Tampa Chamber of Commerce always have had a pool of pretty home-grown young ladies to provide cheesecake for the city's publicity photos. This composite picture has one of the pretty ambassadors relaxing in the grass in Plant Park with an excellent skyline of the city in the background. Photograph by Robertson-Fresh, from the author's collection

A veteran postal figure in Tampa was Samuel G. Harrison, shown here purchasing a newspaper from the shop operated by the blind in the basement of the Federal Building. Harrison started at the bottom and worked his way up the ladder to superintendent of mails and to postmaster. He was one of the first career postal workers to be chosen for the top local post. For many years the postmastership was a political plum awarded to campaign workers. Photograph from the author's collection

Merry X'm
HOLSUM BAKE
Welcome to HOLSUMS
XMAS PARTY
Public

Who can forget those lovely Christ- *mas displays the Holsum Bakers traditionally erected at their bakeries on Hillsborough Avenue back in the 1940s and 1950s? The spectacular lights and animated figures entertained thousands of motorists as they passed as well as the other thousands who stopped to attend the Christmas Party at the plant. Kiddies got little loaves of hot bread to remember the event by. This was the scene at the public party in 1949. Photograph by Robertson-Fresh, from the author's collection*

696

Chapter 6

1950 to Today

In the last three decades or so, Tampa has been a city on the way up, a city whose potential is unlimited. It's fast becoming one of the great commercial centers of the Southeast; a gateway to Latin America; a city of industry, business, tourist attractions, homes, and good living.

In 1950 the U.S. Senate's Kefauver Crime Investigating Committee came to town, ripped into the public officials who permitted gambling and corruption, and left the cleanup to local good citizens.

The geography spread as much land was annexed in the early 1950s. The city sprawled out with suburbia and shopping centers. Downtown suffered but now is making a comeback with a new skyline of glass skyscrapers.

The Tampa Airport is hailed worldwide as probably the finest airport there is. The city has become a sports center with the building of Tampa Stadium and the coming of the Tampa Bay Buccaneers and the Tampa Bay Rowdies soccer team while the Cincinnati Reds baseball club continues to train here. In 1983, the Superbowl was played at Tampa Stadium.

The town is an educational center, too, with the establishment of the University of South Florida and the expansion of the University of Tampa as well as the success of Hillsborough Community College.

Two Interstate highways intersect in Tampa and these, with other expressways, have helped solve the growing traffic problem. But the road-builders are hard-pressed to catch up and keep ahead of the heavy tourist and local traffic. In recent years, the ideal Tampa port has added facilities for cruise ships.

The trend of businesses, manufacturers, and other commercial activities to follow the sun to the United States sun belt has brought Tampa its share of new people and new enterprises. Local government has been revamped and geared up for the new and burgeoning community.

In this last part of the last quarter of the twentieth century, Tampa is alive and well, thank you, and preparing for its role as one of the great cities of the southeastern United States.

(overleaf)
It might be said that this is the world's most photographed vessel. Through two world wars, the Tampa Shipyard turned out fighting ships, many of them earning fame in sea battles. But a unique vessel built by the yards and itself quite famous was not a real warship—it was the Jose Gasparilla, *flagship of Tampa's colorful Ye Mystic Krewe aof Gasparilla. It is the only ship in the world built solely for piratical purposes. A replica of a West Indiaman, vintage 1800, the Krewe vessel is used once a year in February to transport the play-like pirates as they invade Tampa. The* Jose Gasparilla, *seen here escorted by a flotilla of small boats during an invasion, was built during 1953 and 1954 and was commissioned on January 5, 1954. She has a displacement of 300 tons. The overall length is 164 feet, six inches, and she has a 35-foot beam. Three masts tower some 100 feet skyward. Photograph from the author's collection*

Mrs. J. Roy Frierson of Tampa was active in the Daughters of the American Revolution (DAR) at local, state, and national levels for many years. This portrait was taken in 1950 when she was curator-general of the national organization in charge of the museum of Washington, D.C. She served as state regent in 1946. Photograph from the author's collection

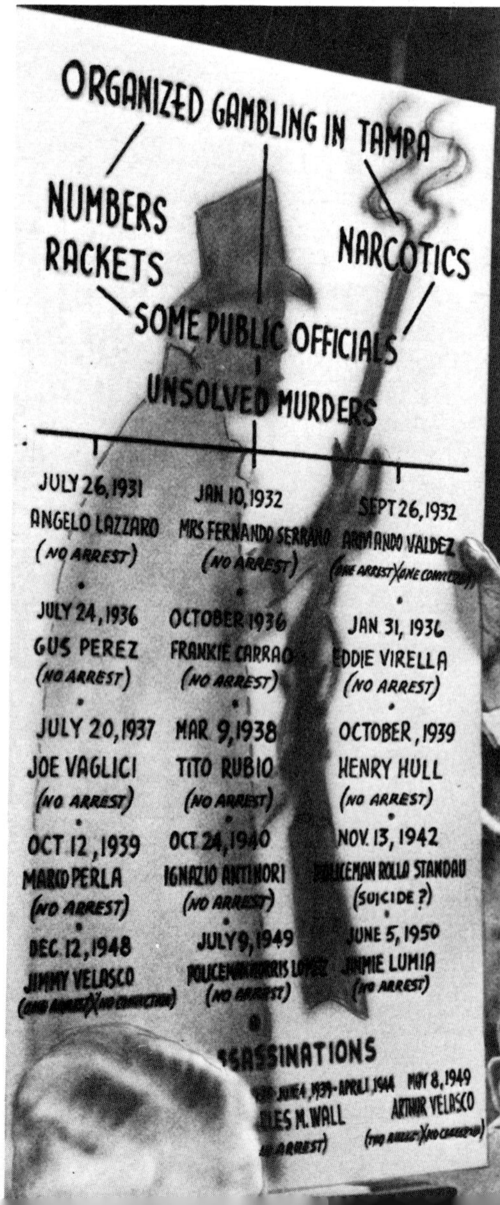

In 1950 an ambitious, personable U.S. senator from Tennessee, Estes Kefauver, a Democrat, was building up an image to run for president of the United States. A springboard he used to grab headlines around the country was to probe organized crime in America. He was chairman of the Senate Special Committee to Investigate Crime in Interstate Commerce from May 10, 1950 to May 1, 1951. So it was that a stop in Tampa was included in the group's barnstorming tour. Kefauver himself did not come here at that time but sent a subcommittee with Senator Lester C. Hunt, Democrat of Wyoming, in the chair. For two or three days, the committee hauled witnesses before it in the Federal Building downtown. Public officials here were the chief targets as the attempt was made to show a link between the officeholders and the underworld. One exhibit during the hearing was a huge poster showing a sinister gangster in the background with a smoking shotgun and listing the unsolved murders reportedly linked to the underworld here. Most of the deaths were recorded in the 1930s when there was a big turnover in the gang situation. The poster is shown in this photo with Senator Hunt in the foreground. Photograph by the Tampa Daily Times, *from the author's collection*

Here are three giants in the sports field. Dining in 1951 at the old Thomas Jefferson Hotel are (left to right) Sol Fleischman, dean of sportscasters in Florida with a long career on radio station WDAE and television station WTVT; former world's heavyweight champion Jack Dempsey; and famed wrestler and promoter Cowboy Luttrall. Photograph by the Tampa Daily Times, *from the author's collection*

The Patrol is a spit-and-polish marching unit of the Egypt Temple Shrine. Here they are all decked out in their handsome uniforms to pose for a picture on October 15, 1951. Photograph from the author's collection

For nearly thirty years, the first thing the readers of the Tampa Morning Tribune *saw when they reached for their daily paper was an excellent cartoon of the day's news. It was drawn by talented, congenial George White. He was an institution. His black and white sketches interpreted the happenings simply and entertainingly. Photograph by the* Tampa Tribune, *from the author's collection*

This original cartoon by George White appeared in the Tampa Morning Tribune *on Armistice Day—November 11th—during the Korean War. White's cartoons were especially welcomed during World War II because he always was depicting the allies as winning the war even though the news reports were gloomy. The* Tribune *reproduced many of his outstanding World War II cartoons in two books entitled* The War in Black With White. *White died in the 1960s and Tribuneland lost a friend and delightful companion. Original cartoon by George White in the* Tampa Morning Tribune, *from the author's collection*

It was a happy day for Tampa on August 17, 1952 when a new terminal was opened at Tampa International Airport. More than 10,000 persons poured onto the field to witness the modern structure. Captain Eddie V. Rickenbacker, aviation pioneer and then president of Eastern Air Lines, spoke at a $3.50 luncheon with items flown in from the Caribbean being served. The terminal cost some $2 million and soon needed expansion. The north concourse was added in 1960-61 and the south concourse was opened in late 1961. And then, in 1971, the most elegant terminal of 'em all was dedicated. Today's Taj Mahal is considered one of the most beautiful airports in the world. The photo of the old terminal was made November 20, 1952. Photograph by Burgert Brothers, from the author's collection

Royalty of Ye Mystic Krewe of Gasparilla in 1952 were King Gilvie L. Reeves, prominent Tampa attorney, and Patricia Lowry (Mrs. Edgar D. Sweeney). Photograph from the author's collection

Tampa falls again to the bloodthirsty pirates of Gasparilla! Mayor Curtis Hixon surrenders the key to the city to Krewe Captain James W. Warren in front of Plant Field grandstand at the Florida State Fair in 1953. Photograph by Robertson-Fresh, from the author's collection

Except for one day in the year, they are sedate Tampa business and professional men. But on Gasparilla Day in February they suddenly become free-spirited, fun-seeking, marauding pirates. Some of the invaders ride triumphantly on their own float into the Florida State Fairgrounds at Plant Field in 1953. Photograph by Robertson-Fresh, from the author's collection

Hello, down there, Tampa! High atop the Thomas Jefferson Hotel at Franklin and Washington streets, this daring duo of dancers wave to a daring photographer as they get ready to perform. That's Franklin Street, looking north. Photograph by Robertson-Fresh, from the author's

The Spanish architecture of the Theodore Roosevelt Elementary School makes for a handsome backdrop as Mrs. Phylis Brulett's junior primary 1 class poses for its official photograph in 1953. Photograph by Robertson-Fresh, from the author's collection

The Hillsborough County Courthouse was sparkling new when this shot was made December 2, 1952. This was the fourth home for county government. At the extreme right is a glimpse of the old Knox Hotel, which faced on Lafayette Street (now Kennedy Boulevard). It later was demolished and an annex was built for the courthouse. Photograph by Robertson-Fresh, from the author's collection

This is the gorgeous facade of the new Hillsborough County Courthouse. This picture was taken April 24, 1953. Photograph by Robertson-Fresh, from the author's collection

A popular dining spot in January 1952 was the Barcelona Spanish Restaurant at 4712-14 Nebraska Avenue. Photograph by Robertson-Fresh, from the author's collection

Law enforcement officers who were members of the Egypt Temple Shrine formed this snappy Provost Guard in 1953. A few who are recognized include John H. Spencer, Horace Locke, Charles Otero, Hampton Murrell, J. D. Latture, and Jack Dempsey. Photograph by Robertson-Fresh, from the author's collection

Public figures were guests on a radio forum over WDAE on March 26, 1953. The moderator was Hampton Dunn, then managing editor and political columnist of the Tampa Daily Times. *His visitors this night were members of the Hillsborough County Legislative delegation. Clockwise from left are Senator John Branch (gesturing with hands); Representative Tom. J. Johnson, Jr.; Dunn; Representative James S. Moody; and Representative Sam M. Gibbons (now congressman). Photograph by the* Tampa Daily Times *from the author's collection*

This tremendous trio of all-star broadcasters was the winning team calling the action of the University of Florida Gators in 1953. From different parts of the state they came together on the weekends to bring the play-by-play and color on the Gator network (left to right): Otis Boggs, Ray Dantzler, and Sol Fleischman. Boggs announced in March 1982 that he was hanging up his mike at Florida Stadium—after thirty-eight years! He continues as sports director of the Gator flagship station, WRUF in Gainesville. Dantzler, then from Jacksonville, for many years now has been on television station WTVT in Tampa and until recently was the editorial voice of the station. Fleischman was dean of Florida sportscasters when he retired a few years ago after more than forty-five years on the air, first at radio station WDAE in Tampa and then for WTVT-TV. He now lives in Sun City Center and Anna Maria Island. Photograph from the author's collection

St. Joseph's Hospital moved into its glistening, huge and handsome plant of Buffalo Avenue in 1961. And it said goodbye to an overcrowded but durable building where it was founded in 1934 at the corner of Morgan Street and Seventh Avenue. The photo shows the hospital in operation at that location in 1954. In the fall of 1933 the Franciscan Sisters of Allegheny, N.Y. acquired a partially furnished four-story building from the Tampa Heights Hospital. After "St. Joe" moved to its new quarters, the old building was operated as St. Elizabeth's Hospital, but this did not last long. The vacant building still stands. Photograph by Burgert Brothers, from the author's collection

Boy power pulled the pleasing floats in the annual Children's Gasparilla Parades staged during the 1940s and 1950s. Junior pirates escort the float bearing the king and queen in 1956, moving snappily down Franklin Street. Photograph by Robertson-Fresh, from the author's collection

A gala function is the annual Election Ball of the Latin American Fiesta. This was the scene the night of March 20, 1954 at Fort Homer Hesterly Armory. The audience feasts as the royal court performs on stage. Photograph from the author's collection

Phillips Field football stadium on the Hillsborough River at Cass Street reverberated with music from hundreds of instruments of high school musicians performing in a massed concert the night of May 4, 1954. Photograph by Robertson-Fresh, from the author's collection

General Carlos Romulo, center, was Philippine Ambassador to the United States in December 1953 when he came here to address the Tampa Executives' Club. He's greeted by Jack D. Peters, left, and Richard D. (Dick) Jackson. Romulo also served as president of the United Nations General Assembly. Photograph courtesy of Richard D. Jackson, from the author's collection

The choir, leaders, and some of the congregation of the Port Tampa Methodist Church pose for the photographer in front of the historic structure on November 20, 1954. The church dates back to the 1890s. Photograph by Robertson-Fresh, from the author's collection

A veteran publisher and editor from the metropolitan newspaper wars of Philadelphia and New York was David E. Smiley, who with his partner, Ralph Nicholson, took over the Tampa Daily Times *in 1933. Smiley subsequently bought out Nicholson and then in 1958 sold the paper to the* Tribune. *The erudite editor is shown at his desk, going over proofs of his hard-hitting editorials. Photograph by the* Tampa Daily Times *from the author's collection*

All decorated for the Gasparilla festivities in the early 1950s is the Tampa Daily Times *building at Franklin and Washington streets. The newspaper was independent and owned radio station WDAE, which had studios in the building. This building was the first brick structure in Tampa, originally housing the Bank of Tampa in the 1880s. In its final years the building housed the Merchants Association of Tampa. It was demolished to make way for the new urban development downtown. The* Times *was sold on June 1, 1958 to its rival, the* Tampa Tribune. *Photograph by the* Tampa Daily Times *from the author's collection*

Tampa housewives may have been fussing about the rising cost of food in June 1954, but nevertheless they were buying coffee for ninety-nine cents a pound, chuck roast at nineteen cents a pound, and other bargains at the grand opening of a B & B Super Market. Photograph by Robertson-Fresh, from the author's collection

One of the major WPA projects in Tampa during the Depression was the construction of a new armory for local units of the Florida National Guard. The structure was named Fort Homer W. Hesterly in 1941 in honor of Colonel Hesterly, who was long active in the artillery service. This photo was taken May 9, 1955. Photograph from the author's collection

Bobby Lord, who made it big in country music on the Grand Ole Opry in Nashville, grew up in Tampa and got his start in the professional entertainment world here. He performed on radio station WDAE and made numerous personal appearances around town. He's shown here belting it out at McKay Auditorium in the early 1950s. He has been back home many times since hitting big time and has often performed at the Florida State Fair. Photograph from the author's collection

Queen Marie Joann Mirabella of Tampa's Latin-American Fiesta and her party appear ready to board a National Air Lines flight for a short hop to our neighboring island of Cuba in February 1956. It was a good-will tour and the Floridians were welcomed in Havana by President Fulgencio Batista. Others in the Queen's entourage were Leon S. Cazin, Sr., founder and leader of the Fiesta; Mrs. Cazin; Leon Cazin, Jr.; Maid Pauline Violet Mistretta; Maid Ida Ann Felicione; Maid Mary Ann Licata; Maid Sylvia Arias; Mrs. Grace Brooks, chaperone; Karl B. Cuesta; Carol O. Gabbert; Mrs. Gabbert; Emilio Cerra; Miss Juanita Juarez; Joseph Mistretta; Mrs. Virginia Mistretta; Mrs. Mary Chamoun; Mrs. Helen Juarez; Harry J. Beecham; Mrs. Ruby M. Beecham; Mrs. Esther Barr; Mr. and Mrs. Karl King; Mr. and Mrs. Lyman Wiltse; Marcelino Huerta; Vince Meloy; Jack Espinosa; Mr. and Mrs. Ostacio Fernandez; Miss Evelyn Faris; Mike Chamoun; and William V. (Red) Robertson, official photographer, who took this picture. Photograph by Robertson-Fresh, from the author's collection

Alfonso Raymond (Al) Lopez, a product of Ybor City's sandlot baseball, became the first Tampa native to make the major leagues, and he was among the first Florida-grown national sports celebrities. Tampa Tribune *Sports Editor Tom McEwen calls him "Dale Carnegie in Pinstripes"; he's such a nice guy with so many friends everywhere. Still living here, Lopez received the ultimate honor in baseball when he was elected to the game's Hall of Fame at Cooperstown, New York on August 8, 1977. The citation: "Alfonso Ramon Lopez. Renowned for shrewd leadership during 36-year big league career as catcher and manager. Won two pennants and had ten second place finishes with winning percentage of .581 in 17 seasons. At helm of Cleveland and Chicago White sox, only manager to interrupt Yankees' pennant dynasty of 1949-1964, guiding Indians to '54 flag with A. L. record 111 wins and piloting White Sox to 1959 title. Born Aug. 20, 1908, at Tampa, Fla. Elected to Hall of Fame in 1977." This picture shows Lopez, right, and his long-time pal, Sol Fleischman, WDAE sportscaster, in 1955. Photograph by the* Tampa Daily Times *from the author's collection*

Several of the participants in the Florida Senior Golf Association's fourth annual Championship Tournament await their turn to tee off at Palma Ceia Golf and Country Club in February 1956. Photograph by Robertson-Fresh, from the author's collection

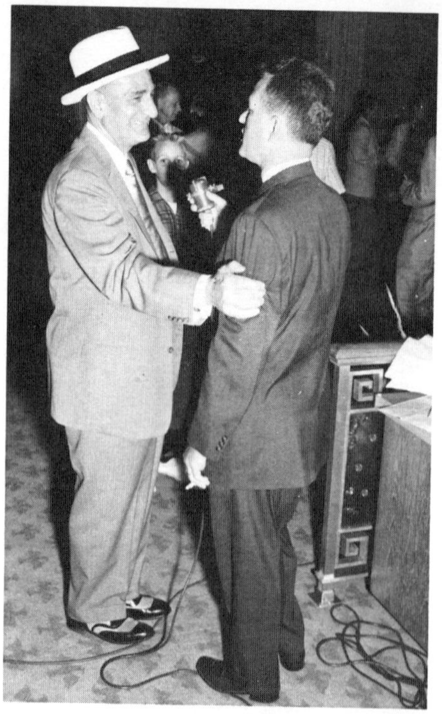

The last hurrah: Nick C. Nuccio is the last of the old-style, favor-doing, ward-heeling type of politician. Now around eighty years old, Nuccio was turned out to pasture a few years ago when Tampa elected handsome, young, smart Dick Greco as mayor in 1967. A native of Ybor City, Nuccio is an eighth-grade dropout. But he has left his mark on the sands and sidewalks of time here as long-time county commissioner, city councilman, and mayor. He was the last of-the-last-hurrah type of mayor who politicked around the clock, did favors for everyone who asked, who was a doer in carrying out big assignments for the city, and who cultivated ethnic groups and the masses of cracker folk alike. He's shown here being interviewed by a broadcaster and turning on the charm. Photograph from the author's collection

Battery A of Tampa's 116th Field Artillery Battalion proudly sat for this official portrait in 1956. It was taken at Fort Homer W. Hesterly Armory, which also is a sports arena. Photograph by Robertson-Fresh, from the author's collection

In 1956, when the integration battle was at its hottest, Tampa's Lieutenant General Sumter L. Lowry ran for governor of Florida on a one-plank segregation platform. He was defeated by the incumbent, Governor LeRoy Collins. In his memoirs Lowry wrote: "My ONE campaign issue was 'Preserve the 10th Ammendment and save your freedom and liberty.' I was defeated . . . The people just could not believe or realize that what I had to say could possibly come true. But, subsequent events have proved me to be right." Candidate Lowry is shown speaking at the Tampa Daily Times-*WDAE Radio Rally. Also in the photo to the right is Elbert Moore, county democratic party chairman. Lowry also ran for Congress in 1962, losing to Sam Gibbons. Photograph by the* Tampa Daily Times *from the author's collection*

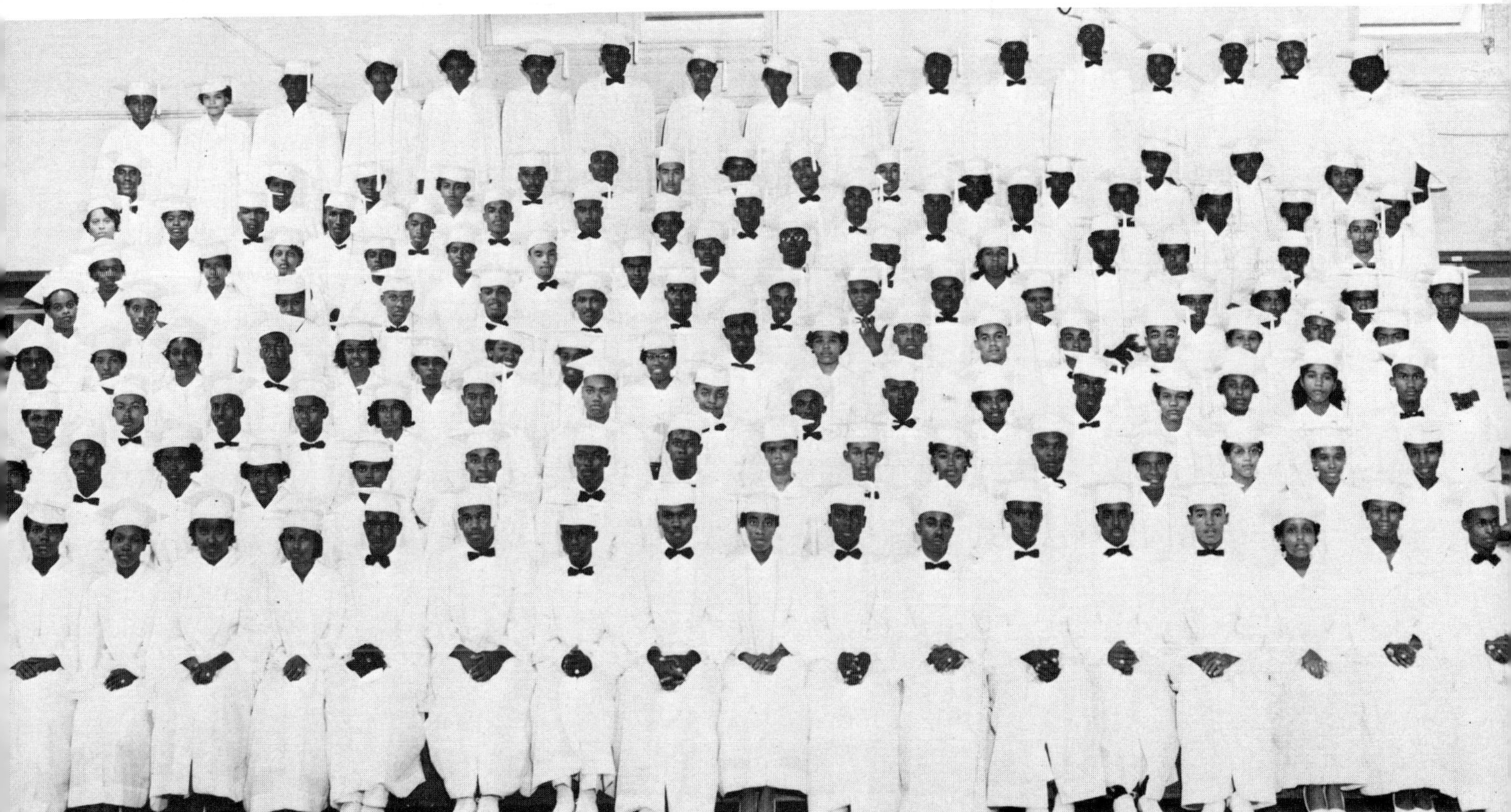

Middleton Senior High School at 4302 Twenty-fourth Street was an all-black school when this class was graduated in 1956. Garland V. Stewart was principal. Photograph by Robertson-Fresh, from the author's collection

It was a brighter Tampa the night of September 29, 1956 when they turned on the modern lighting system on Franklin Street, seen here looking south from about Polk Street. Photograph from the author's collection

During World War II this area in northeast Tampa was the Henderson Air Field used by the air force. The large acreage became an industrial park soon after the war. It now has large breweries and many other huge industries. This picture was made on August 14, 1958 when construction was just beginning. Photograph by Burgert Brothers, from the author's collection

Tampa gained its own state university by action of the 1955 legislature—an event that was to bring tremendous cultural, educational, and economic impact on the community. The daddy and first president of the University of South Florida was Dr. John S. Allen, who became founding president in 1957, presided at the groundbreaking a year later, and greeted the first students in 1960. One of the early students is seen walking across the campus. Photograph from the author's collection

It's gone fancy now and is a refined restaurant and lounge, attracting older people, but for four decades The Colonnade at 3401 Bayshore Boulevard was a classy drive-in that catered to the high school set, especially those from Plant High nearby. The institution was built in 1935 by Dick Whiteside and the building has been remodeled three times. Whiteside died in March 1982. Photograph by Burgert Brothers,

A distinguished Tampa lawyer, Cody Fowler, served as president of the American Bar Association in 1950-51. A native of Tennessee, he had lived here since 1924. He headed the law firm of Fowler, White, Gillen, Boggs, Villareal, and Banker. The attorney's mother, Mrs. Maud Cody Fowler, was one of the founders and developers of Temple Terrace. The former ABA chief had been active in numerous civic, fraternal, and charitable organizations before his death a few years ago. Photograph by Burgert Brothers, from the author's collection

Pretty as a picture is Miss Tampa—1961, Jean Marie "Sammye" Cold, seen here the night of her coronation. Photograph courtesy of George Sanders

As a boy, Doyle E. Carlton, Jr., lived in the Executive Mansion in Tallahassee with his family. His father, Doyle E., Sr., was governor from 1929-33. But young Doyle grew up in Tampa and attended Plant High School and the University of Florida. After service in the air force, he returned to the Carlton family original homesite area in Hardee County and became a rancher and farmer. He also today heads the Havatampa Corporation in Tampa. Young Carlton served two terms in the state senate, and in 1940 ran for the Democratic nomination for governor. In a field of ten candidates, he went into the run-off with Farris Bryant trailing him by only 7,000 votes. But in the second primary, Bryant defeated Carlton by a vote of 512,757 to 415,052. Carlton is married to the former Miss Mildred Woodbery, his high school sweetheart, daughter of Mr. and Mrs. D. Hoyt Woodbery. Photograph by C. Verne Klintworth, from the author's collection

U.S. Senator Spessard L. Holland, left, chats which Joseph T. Lykes, head of the vast Lykes Brothers empire, at an event here on December 8, 1960. Photograph from the author's collection

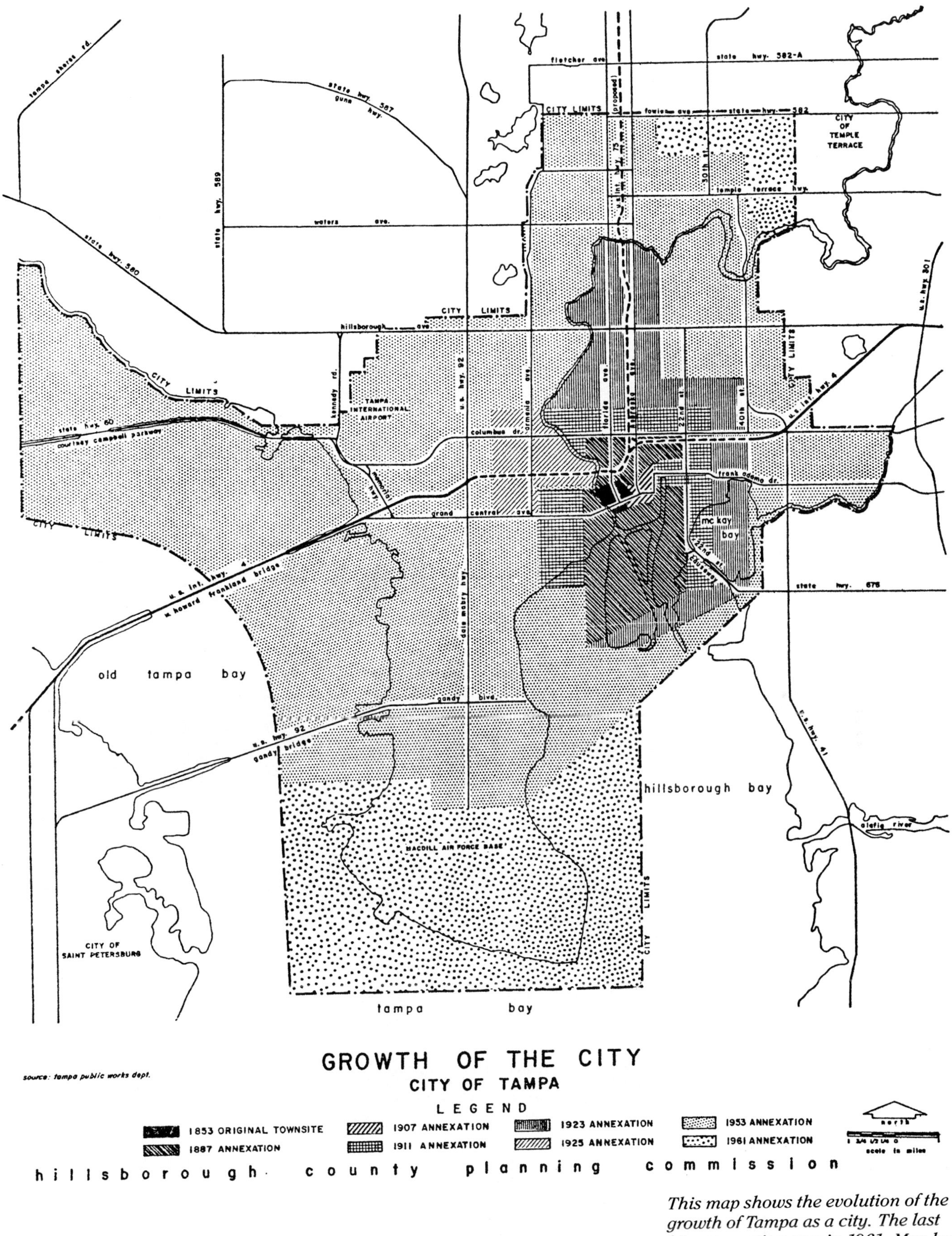

This map shows the evolution of the growth of Tampa as a city. The last big annexation was in 1961. Map by Hillsborough County Planning Commission, from the author's collection

Sporting a crew cut, dark suit, and briefcase, Tampa's Congressman Sam M. Gibbons struts proudly in front of the nation's Capitol as he checks in for duty for his first term in January 1963. A native Tampan, Gibbons was a graduate of the University of Florida and was a paratrooper hero in World War II. He served six years in the Florida House of Representatives and four years in the state senate before becoming a congressman. He has been reelected since his first election. Photograph from the author's collection

Motorists traveling Interstate 275, Florida Avenue or Nebraska Avenue in the north end of the city can't miss a familiar landmark—the Sulphur Springs water tower. It was built in 1927 by the area developer Josiah Richardson, whose motto was "Josiah Knows Where Money Grows." A tank near the top of the 225-foot height is still used to store artesian well water. The old tower has been suggested for many uses through the years such as part of a motel, restaurant, or—a gambling hall. Photograph by the author

A Christmas tradition that started in the Carrollwood subdivision shortly after it opened in the early 1960s is the luminaria on Christmas Eve. Promptly at seven o'clock, residents light up candles in paper sacks spaced ten feet apart along the curbs throughout the neighborhood. The idea was proposed to the Carrollwood Civic Association by Mrs. John S. Allen, wife of the first president of the University of South Florida. The street lamps are doused while the candles burn for several hours and neighbors walk up and down the streets and exchange season's greetings. Photograph from the author's collection

From the paddleball courts of Ybor City's Cuscaden Park to center court of Wimbleton was the very long trek made by Tampa's Judy Alvarez. She's shown here boarding the plane for England in 1963 for her first appearance in Wimbleton. In her second appearance there the following year, she beat Virginia Wade. She also has won over Billy Jean King during her spectacular tennis career. She still competes in the Over-35 Division and ranks at the top of the heap. Judy also operates a Club Tennis in northwest Hillsborough County; it is a thriving center of physical activity and instruction. Photograph from the author's collection

Johns Committee Report Hits Some Activities at USF

Cites Attitudes Toward Religion, Communism, Sex

By TOM O'CONNOR
Tribune Staff Writer

A report critical of several activities at the University of South Florida by the state legislative investigations committee was turned over to the State Board of Control yesterday.

Johns

The committee made an investigation at the Tampa school last spring. Dr. John S. Allen, president, and members of the faculty were questioned extensively.

The 53-page report, which was also presented to Gov. Farris Bryant and the cabinet board of education, delves into teaching methods at the university in the fields of communism and religion and also into obscenity in required and recommended reading, and homosexuality.

Complete text of the Johns' Committee report on University of South Florida, with certain obscenities deleted, starts on Page 10-A.

Months of Study

The report was presented by

In 1962, a Florida legislative committee called the Johns Committee after its chairman, State Senator Charley Johns of Starke (who had been acting governor for a brief time in the mid-1950s), shook up the campus of Tampa's University of South Florida. The lawmakers were seeking to ferret out suspected Communists, homosexuals, and immoral persons. The committee report admitted it found little evidence of ideological and moral aberrations, but it nevertheless expounded at length on readings, speakers, personal and group activities, and free-wheeling classroom discussions considered socially, politically, or morally objectionable. The committee did publish an explicitly illustrated report of sexual aberrations, which a history of USF declares was a "purple pamphlet" that became "a prized item for collectors of pornography." Clipping in the Tampa Tribune, *from the author's collection*

Movie and swim star Esther Williams (right) and her husband, Ben Gage (center, back row) dined at Ybor City's famed Columbia Restaurant one evening in 1965. The celebrity is seated by Mrs. Adela Gonzmart, wife of the present owner and daughter of one of the founders of the Columbia. At left rear is her husband, Cesar Gonzmart, who also tops the entertainment bill at the restaurant. At right rear is the omnipresent Sol Fleischman, veteran radio and television broadcaster. Photograph by Simon's Studio, from the author's collection

Rick Casares Talks About Suspension. Shufelt Column, Page 12

The Tampa Times

The Weather: Rain. High 78, Low 67 (Weather Map, Page 3)

SEVENTY-FOURTH YEAR—No. 49 TAMPA, FLORIDA, MONDAY, APRIL 4, 1966 PRICE FIVE CENTS

Killer Tornado Rips Tampa

At Carrollwood new model car is blown over onto top of dwelling that is destroyed.

At Least 3 Dead; Damage—Millions

Tornado Toll At-a-Glance

Riverview Hard-Hit by Slamming Storm

HELICOPTER VIEW

Worst Ever, Says Veteran Cameraman

'Never Saw Anything Like It'

Tornado Packed Punch at USF

INSIDE

More tornado photos are in today's Times on pages 4, 8 and 9

Inside The Times

Part of Carrollwood toll. Wrecked cars lie among wreckage of home at Lake Carroll Way and Orange Way Drive in Carrollwood.

An unexpected Kansas-like tornado ripped through the Carrollwood subdivision the morning of April 4, 1966. It left a path of destruction across a wide swath of Carrollwood, hopped over to Florida Avenue, even got as far as Lakeland and beyond. This was the front page of the Tampa Times *the afternoon of the disaster. Photograph from the author's collection*

Neighbors, the Red Cross, sheriff's deputies, and others join in the clean-up of damage wreaked by the April 4, 1966 tornado. This was the scene at the author's home at 10610 Carrollwood Drive at Korina Lane shortly after the vicious blow. Three members of the family were in the house when the tornado struck, but fortunately no one was hurt. The tornado lifted much of the roof, ripped away the carport, destroyed the utility room, blew out many windows including a sliding glass door at the rear and picture windows in front, ruined all the furnishings, and blew over numerous tall pine trees onto the building. Other Carrollwood homes were damaged much worse, some totally wiped out. Photograph by Sandy Gandy

Brenda Forbes, 4-H Club member, sold her Black Angus steer at the annual Florida Fat Stock Show and Sale at the Florida State Fair in 1966. It was bought by Richard D. (Dick) Jackson. Official Florida State Fair photograph by Al Major, from the author's collection

It was truly a historic day in September 1966 when pretty Miss Interstate 75 of St. Petersburg snipped the ribbon that opened the superhighway into Tampa at Bearss Avenue. The beauty was Miss Suzanne Warner. Sharing honors at the happy occasion were Vincent Nuccio (left), of Tampa, member of the State Road Board under Governor Haydon Burns, and Floyd Bowen of Lakeland, chairman of the SRB. This link connected Tampa with the main line of the nationwide network, with I-75 going all the way through to Sault Ste. Marie, Michigan. Photograph from the author's collection

What started in 1959 as a beautification project for the grounds and as a hospitality center for the Anheuser-Busch Brewery in Tampa has turned out to be one of the most popular of Florida's attractions—Busch Gardens. Hundreds of wild animals roam freely in the massive African veldt at the gardens. Visitors also can tour by train, skyride, or monorail. Big game is one of many attractions at The Dark Continent, Florida's second most visited theme park. Photograph by the Florida Department of Commerce, from the author's collection

During a visit to Tampa on November 18, 1963, President John F. Kennedy made what turned out to be his last public address. Four days later, he was assassinated in Dallas, Texas. Today at the entrance to the University of Tampa and Plant Park stands an attractive monument honoring the late president. A local committee headed by Robert Florio financed the memorial by public subscription. Sculptor Bernherdt Zuckerman of New York and Italy did the high relief sculpture on a slab of white Carrara marble. The backdrop is of black pearl granite. The memorial was dedicated on May 30, 1966 by U.S. Congressman Sam Gibbons of Tampa, a close friend of the president. City Council changed the names of Lafayette Street and much of Grand Central Avenue to John F. Kennedy Boulevard. Photograph by the author

The incumbent and a former chief executive had a warm meeting when they came together at the dedication of the new Tampa International Airport terminal on April 14, 1971. That's Governor Reuben Askew on the left and former Governor Doyle E. Carlton, Sr., of Tampa, on the right. Governor Carlton died in October 1972 at the age of eighty-five. He served from 1929-1933. Askew served two four-year terms as governor and in 1984 was a Democratic candidate for president of the United States. Photograph by Sandy Gandy, from the author's collection

Donning her regal trappings, beautiful Miss Bonnie McGregor takes over as Miss Tampa of 1970. Photograph from the author's collection

On August 9, 1971 Robert (Bo) Gray had an unusually busy day: (1) he celebrated his nineteenth birthday, (2) he registered for the draft, (3) he registered to vote, and (4) he filed as a candidate for the Tampa City Council. This was the first year the voting age had been lowered from 21 to 18 and this alert lad was ready for action. He ran third. A Hillsborough Community College student at the time, Bo subsequently earned a Bachelor of Science degree in broadcasting from the University of Florida, worked for a number of years as sports writer for the Tampa Times, *and recently graduated as a divinity student at Trinity College in Chicago. Now a minister in Lynchburg, Virginia, he is married and a young father of two. Photograph by Simon's Studio, from the author's collection*

The Tampa Airport Marriott Hotel, located as the centerpiece in the magnificent Tampa International Airport, is one of the assets that make the Tampa airport a monument of convenience in air transportation. Photograph courtesy of Greater Tampa Chamber of Commerce from the author's collection

Dana Greco, lovely first lady to Mayor Dick A. Greco, carefully christens an airplane of radio station WDAE to be used in traffic spotting. The mayor looks on approvingly. The ceremony took place at Peter O. Knight Airport in the early 1970s. Al Ford has become a familiar figure around town as he broadcasts his frequent traffic reports daily. He moved to radio station WSUN in 1984. Photograph by Ted Saylor, from the author's collection

For five years in the 1970s, Dr. Maurice Cecil Mackey was the high-powered—and controversial—president of the University of South Florida. He succeeded the charter president, Dr. John S. Allen, in February 1971 and served until the summer of 1976 when he went to Lubbock, Texas to accept the presidency of Texas Tech. At one time prior to coming here, Dr. Mackey was executive vice president of Florida State University and later assistant secretary of the U.S. Department of Transportation in Washington. USF went through a rapid growth period while he was president. It was during this time the big medical center and a new library were added to the sprawling campus. This picture was taken in 1976 at the AAA Transportation Forum in Orlando. Photograph from the author's collection

From 1968 to 1970, Lieutenant General Benjamin O. Davis, Jr., was deputy commander-in-chief of the U.S. Strike Command at MacDill Air Force Base in Tampa. After retirement, he was named in April 1975 as special assistant to Secretary of Transportation William T. Coleman, Jr., in charge of the fifty-five-mile-an-hour speed limit program. Official photograph of the U.S. Department of Transportation, from the author's collection

Citrus Park Elementary School has captured a part of American heritage most other schools can only offer through the glossy pages of a history book. Nestled beside the sprawling, more modern school buildings is a 1911 one-room red schoolhouse. Patrons of the school battled forces trying to transfer the historic structure to the Florida State Fairgrounds in 1975 and won. A class of twenty-seven fifth-graders uses the schoolhouse every day, studying in an atmosphere much like their ancestors experienced seventy-four years ago. Photograph from the author's collection

Tampan Kathleen Griffith captured the title Miss World Airlines in 1971, thus being recognized as the world's most beautiful air stewardess. The 1965 graduate of Brewster Vocational School, who was flying for Eastern Airlines, was chosen from more than 400 entrants in the contest sponsored by Varig Airlines and Rio de Janeiro's Hotel Gloria. Kathleen is pictured at Tampa International Airport. Photograph from the author's collection

Freddie Solomon dazzled defenses and excited University of Tampa Spartans football fans as UT's quarterback in the school's last days of the grid sport 1972-75. He's shown here (No. 3) playing against Toledo in 1974. He was hyped for the Heisman trophy but failed to win it. Today, Solomon is wide receiver for the Super Bowl Champion San Francisco Forty-Niners and starred in the showdown with Cincinnati in January 1982, and in his team's victory in the 1985 Super Bowl. He was named Professional Athlete of the Year in 1981 by the Tampa Sports Club. Tampa U. dropped football when Solomon graduated. Quipped Spartan-supporter Michel Emmanuel: "Freddie was so good and so outstanding when he finished college, the University of Tampa retired the sport [football]." Photograph from the author's collection

Gerald Ford was "only" vice president in 1974 when he addressed the University of Tampa, but he soon became president of the United States. Standing second from left is Dr. Bob Owens, president of the University at the time. Photograph from the author's collection

Gordon Jago was the affable coach of the Tampa Bay Rowdies from 1978 until he resigned suddenly in the middle of the 1982 season. The St. Petersburg Times reported Jago "led the Rowdies to the brink of both glory and disaster" in his five years' tenure. Jago himself said, "I'm very lucky. I've been to two Soccer Bowls and had an indoor championship." He was retained on the administrative staff, but later moved away. Photograph by Richard Steinmetz, from the author's collection

Soccer became a popular professional—and amateur—sport almost overnight in Tampa in 1974 when George Strawbridge, Jr., Philadelphia businessman, was awarded the franchise for the Tampa Bay Rowdies. This photo shows NASL All-Star Mike Connell and teammate Zeljko Bilechi in action against the Detroit Express. Connell was the youngest defender named to the first team in 1979. Photograph by DuCharme, from the author's collection

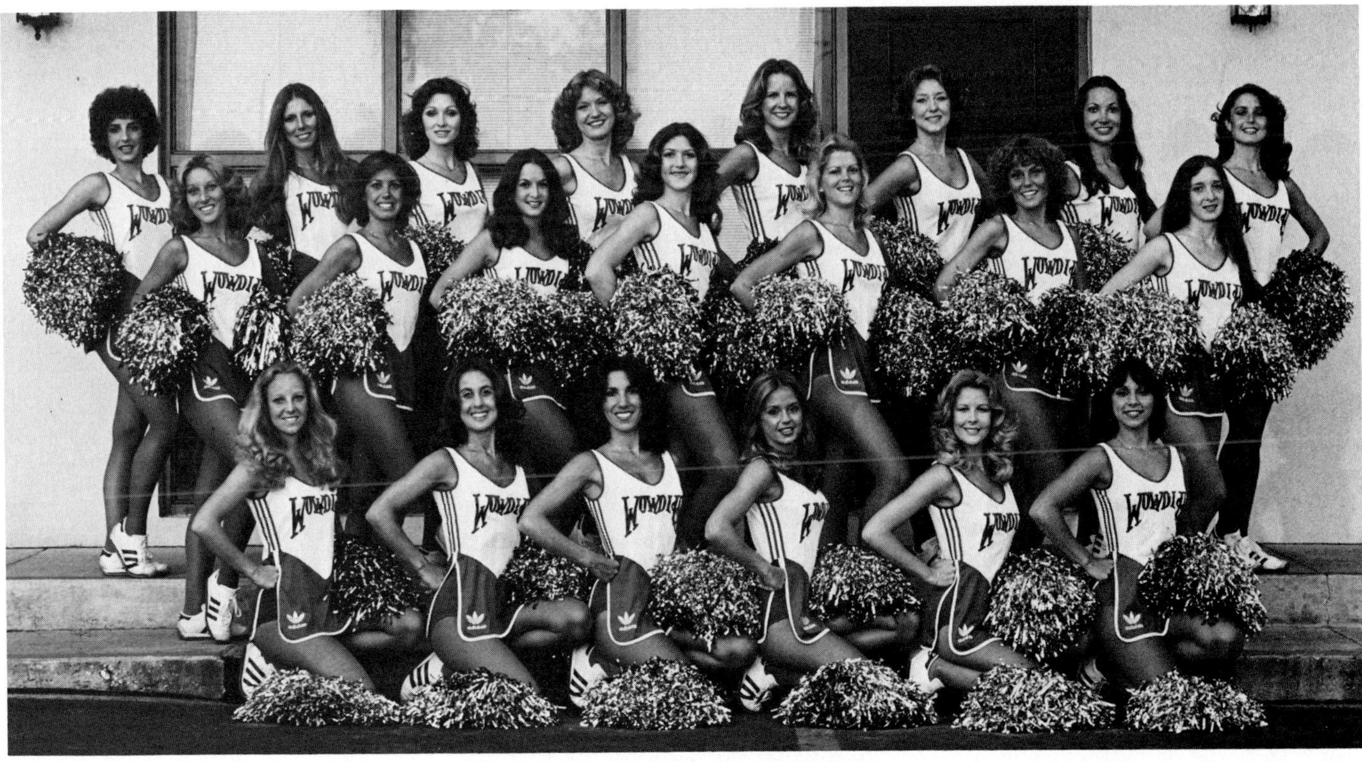

With this corps of beauties supporting them, how can the Tampa Bay Rowdies lose? The cheerleaders are called Wowdies and Tampa Bay fans are labeled Fannies. This photo was taken May 22, 1979. Photograph by Richard Steinmetz, from the author's collection

Tampa went big time in the sports world in 1975 when the Tampa Bay Buccaneers was fielded at Tampa Stadium. This is an action shot of an early team. Photograph by Florida News Bureau, Department of Commerce, from the author's collection

Coach John McKay appeared perfectly contented smoking his Tampa-made cigar and thinking about winning more games and honors with his Tampa Bay Buccaneers when this photo was taken in April 1982. But in 1984 he resigned as head coach and was appointed president of the club by owner Hugh Culverhouse. Early in January 1985, McKay's coaching duties were assumed by Leeman Bennett, former head coach of the Atlanta Falcons. So long, Coach McKay; good luck, President McKay! Photograph by Fred Fox, the Tampa Times, from the author's collection

Tampa businessman Hugh F. Culverhouse is owner of the Tampa Bay Buccaneers. Photograph from the author's collection

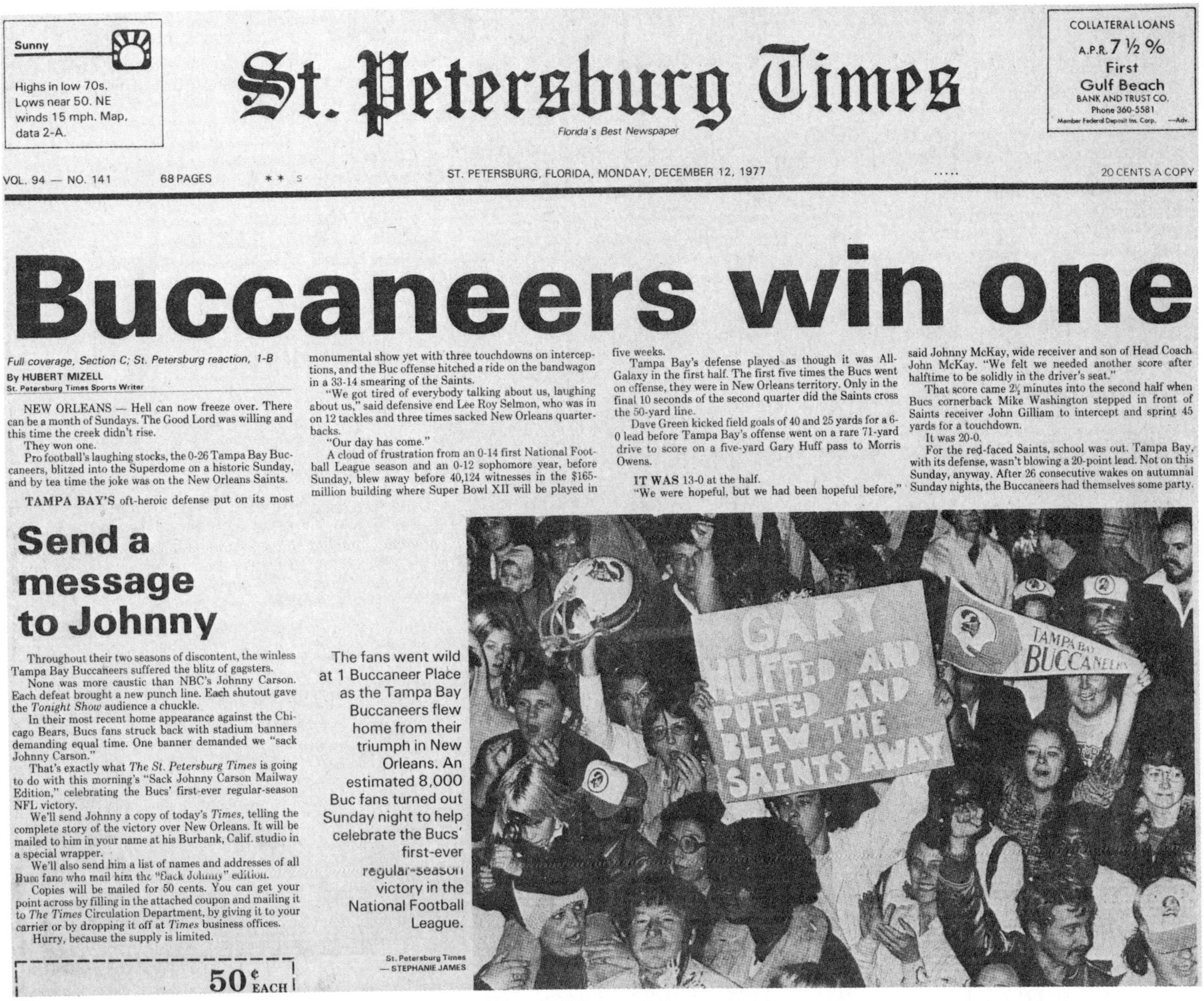

Sunny

Highs in low 70s. Lows near 50. NE winds 15 mph. Map, data 2-A.

St. Petersburg Times

Florida's Best Newspaper

COLLATERAL LOANS A.P.R. 7 ½ % First Gulf Beach BANK AND TRUST CO. Phone 360-5581 Member Federal Deposit Ins. Corp. —Adv.

VOL. 94 — NO. 141 68 PAGES * * S ST. PETERSBURG, FLORIDA, MONDAY, DECEMBER 12, 1977 ..... 20 CENTS A COPY

Buccaneers win one

Full coverage, Section C; St. Petersburg reaction, 1-B

By HUBERT MIZELL
St. Petersburg Times Sports Writer

NEW ORLEANS — Hell can now freeze over. There can be a month of Sundays. The Good Lord was willing and this time the creek didn't rise.

They won one.

Pro football's laughing stocks, the 0-26 Tampa Bay Buccaneers, blitzed into the Superdome on a historic Sunday, and by tea time the joke was on the New Orleans Saints.

TAMPA BAY'S oft-heroic defense put on its most monumental show yet with three touchdowns on interceptions, and the Buc offense hitched a ride on the bandwagon in a 33-14 smearing of the Saints.

"We got tired of everybody talking about us, laughing about us," said defensive end Lee Roy Selmon, who was in on 12 tackles and three times sacked New Orleans quarterbacks.

"Our day has come."

A cloud of frustration from an 0-14 first National Football League season and an 0-12 sophomore year, before Sunday, blew away before 40,124 witnesses in the $165-million building where Super Bowl XII will be played in five weeks.

Tampa Bay's defense played as though it was All-Galaxy in the first half. The first five times the Bucs went on offense, they were in New Orleans territory. Only in the final 10 seconds of the second quarter did the Saints cross the 50-yard line.

Dave Green kicked field goals of 40 and 25 yards for a 6-0 lead before Tampa Bay's offense went on a rare 71-yard drive to score on a five-yard Gary Huff pass to Morris Owens.

IT WAS 13-0 at the half.

"We were hopeful, but we had been hopeful before," said Johnny McKay, wide receiver and son of Head Coach John McKay. "We felt we needed another score after halftime to be solidly in the driver's seat."

That score came 2½ minutes into the second half when Bucs cornerback Mike Washington stepped in front of Saints receiver John Gilliam to intercept and sprint 45 yards for a touchdown.

It was 20-0.

For the red-faced Saints, school was out. Tampa Bay, with its defense, wasn't blowing a 20-point lead. Not on this Sunday, anyway. After 26 consecutive wakes on autumnal Sunday nights, the Buccaneers had themselves some party.

Send a message to Johnny

Throughout their two seasons of discontent, the winless Tampa Bay Buccaneers suffered the blitz of gagsters.

None was more caustic than NBC's Johnny Carson. Each defeat brought a new punch line. Each shutout gave the *Tonight Show* audience a chuckle.

In their most recent home appearance against the Chicago Bears, Bucs fans struck back with stadium banners demanding equal time. One banner demanded we "sack Johnny Carson."

That's exactly what *The St. Petersburg Times* is going to do with this morning's "Sack Johnny Carson Mailway Edition," celebrating the Bucs' first-ever regular-season NFL victory.

We'll send Johnny a copy of today's *Times*, telling the complete story of the victory over New Orleans. It will be mailed to him in your name at his Burbank, Calif. studio in a special wrapper.

We'll also send him a list of names and addresses of all Bucs fans who mail him the "Sack Johnny" edition.

Copies will be mailed for 50 cents. You can get your point across by filling in the attached coupon and mailing it to *The Times* Circulation Department, by giving it to your carrier or by dropping it off at *Times* business offices.

Hurry, because the supply is limited.

50¢ EACH

The fans went wild at 1 Buccaneer Place as the Tampa Bay Buccaneers flew home from their triumph in New Orleans. An estimated 8,000 Buc fans turned out Sunday night to help celebrate the Bucs' first-ever regular-season victory in the National Football League.

St. Petersburg Times — STEPHANIE JAMES

After twenty-six straight winless games, the Tampa Bay Buccaneers got into the victory column in New Orleans' Superdome on December 11, 1977. Hubert Mizell, sports editor of the St. Petersburg Times, *said it all when the lead on his story (which was the lead story on page one, not the sports page) read: "Hell can now freeze over. There can be a month of Sundays. The Good Lord is willing and this time the creek didn't rise. They won one. Pro football's laughing stocks, the 0-26 Tampa Bay Buccaneers, blitzed into the Superdome on a historic Sunday, and by tea time the joke was on the New Orleans' Saints." Tampa Bay, 33; Saints, 14. Front page of the* St. Petersburg Times, *from the author's collection*

Tampa's Big Daddy Don Garlits is many times national champion drag racer. He's shown here in his 1978 Top Fuel dragster powered by a 2,000 horsepower Dodge engine. Garlits is holder of the world record on the quarter-mile, clocking from zero to 250.69 miles per hour in 5.63 seconds! Photograph from the author's collection

It really did. It snowed in Tampa on Tuesday, January 19, 1977! The white stuff started just before daybreak and continued for several hours. It stuck to the ground and did not melt until midmorning. The Weather Bureau reported the temperature was thirty-seven degrees, one degree below the level for snow, and the humidity was eighty percent—the conditions were "just right." The entire front page of the Tampa Times *that afternoon was devoted to the big snow story. Front page of the* Tampa Times *from the author's collection*

The Tampa Times

84th Year — No. 298 | Tampa, Florida, Wednesday, January 19, 1977 | 48 Pages—10 Cents —Home Edition

Snow stuns Tampans

Snow Quotes

Times staff reports

He can't stay

"I'm from New York and I moved down here to get away from it. I guess I'll have to go to the Equator" — Tampa police officer S.L. Dunlap.

A day for play

"Everybody went home to play in the snow today and nobody's working" — Tom Hoyt, construction superintendent.

A new delight

"I've lived here 18 years and I've never seen anything like it" — Fred Skettini, 19, Tampa.

A crazy sight

"Crazy...I wish it would do it every year around Christmas" — Mike Herrick, truck driver for Sealtest.

Disbelief

"I don't believe it" — a local man who drove 1,700 miles to Cherokee, N.C., a week ago to show his wife and children snow, upon awakening this morning in snowy Tampa.

It's really neat

"I've never seen snow before. It's really neat" — Don Grace, 22, of 4020 River Place.

Lovable, too

"We love it" — Pamela Chavez, 17.

Couldn't wait

"I was so excited. I was in my pajamas and I ran outside. I was barefoot and running in the snow" — Amy Newman, student.

Driver loses battle with ice

Don Foger/TAMPA TIMES

This overturned car lying in an icy ditch on Fletcher Avenue in north Tampa offers evidence, repeated many times around the community today, of the hectic traffic problems created by the unexpected northern-style weather. Ice-slick bridges were a major cause of skids and accidents on expressways in the area.

Times Staff Report

It was snowing in Tampa this morning, to the delight of youngsters who played in the white stuff and built snowmen and the dismay of motorists whose cars were sliding on icy roads.

About 175 traffic accidents sent some 58 persons to local hospitals, causing the death of one man today.

Several local schools were forced to close.

The Florida Highway Patrol closed Interstate 4 and Interstate 275 from about 7:30 a.m. until 10:30 a.m. because of snow and icy conditions, a spokesman for the patrol said.

Reports from east Hillsborough County indicate the snow and ice which powdered the area overnight may have completely killed the first phase of strawberry season.

"It looks bad, real bad," said Springhead berry grower Carl Grooms. "It snowed four hours out here."

"I figure we'll lose all the first bloom 100 per cent," said Dover farmer Herbert Hare. "This is going to throw us that much further behind."

Three schools lost electrical power and the second sessions of all double session schools were canceled because of the weather today, school officals said.

More snow photos, stories, pages 14, 15A

Paul Wharton, assistant school superintendent for administration, said Plant City High School, George Washington Junior High and Graham Elementary were without heat, but power was expected to have been restored by noon.

Second sessions of six schools were canceled because additional cold weather is expected to hit Tampa about 4 p.m., said Larry Wagers, director of administration for the school system.

The six schools are Webb and Dowdell Junior Highs and Leto, King, Brandon, and East Bay High Schools.

Parents should use their judgment on deciding whether to send children to school, but any student missing class would be excused, school officials said.

School officials said it would be late this afternoon before they decide whether schools will be open tomorrow.

Water pipes in local homes may freeze tonight if the home is built above ground, says the director of the Tampa water department.

Dave Tippin suggested residents could prevent water from freezing in the pipes by keeping a small stream of water running.

He said he was not concerned about this happening in homes built on concrete slabs; only homes built above the ground could be affected.

Tampa Electric Co. was forced to cut back service to many areas of the bay area at about 7 a.m. today because it was unable to meet the demand for power caused by cold

Ice creates chaos on bay area roads

By BARBARA REICHLE and LORI ANN HAUBENSTOCK
Times Staff Writers

"Once upon a time it snowed in Tampa ... and all hell broke loose."

That's what one Tampa police captain said early today as reports of about 175 multiple car accidents kept pouring in over the police radio and telephone.

The excitement of the white winter ended early this morning for 58 persons who were taken to the emergency rooms of three Tampa hospitals.

All 58 persons suffered injuries in traffic accidents resulting from icy roads, hospital officials said.

By 8:45 a.m. Interstate 275 and Interstate 4 were closed off to north-south and east-west traffic by the

Bibelhauser fell approximately 35 feet, and was rushed to Tampa General Hospital, where he died shortly afterwards.

There were two reports of accidents involving school buses; one in Tampa and one in Brandon.

There were no serious injuries in either accident. The school bus accident in Brandon occurred on State Road 574 near Parsons Avenue, said a spokesman for the county sheriff's office.

The school bus accident in Tampa occurred about 8 a.m. at Orient Road near Adamo Drive.

Tampa police chief Charles Otero said there were an additional 30 patrolmen on the streets early today investigating accidents.

"Cracker Country," located within the Florida State Fairgrounds, recreates turn-of-the-century rural Florida and now contains two homes and the Okahumpka Railroad Depot, all of which have been moved from their permanent sites and are being restored. Also added have been a small church and a one-room schoolhouse. One of the rural homes is the birthplace of former Governor Doyle E. Carlton, Sr., and was moved from Wauchula. Photograph courtesy of Greater Tampa Chamber of Commerce, from the author's collection

A seasoned winner of beauty contests, Carolyn Cline had a particularly big year in 1978. She was chosen Miss Tampa, then Miss Florida, and went on to become second runner-up to Miss America. Miss Cline surrendered her Miss Florida title so she could pursue her singing career full time. Accompanying herself on the piano, she has sung Top 40 and country and Western songs from Tokyo to Las Vegas, the Philippines, and Hong Kong. Photograph from the author's collection

During the period from 1973 to 1980, the University of South Florida campaigned for funds to acquire the world's largest Pablo Picasso sculpture. The idea of this artwork on USF campus created a huge hassle in the city, but the funds never were forthcoming. The sculpture, called Bust of a Woman, *was to stand nearly eleven stories tall. It was to be made of concrete and steel coated with an outerfinish of Alabama quartzite river pebble—an off-white color with a sprinkling of pink and gray. While some mourned the loss because it might have put Tampa and USF on the world's cultural forefront, others were relieved the campus would not be home to what they described as a 110-foot tall "pigeon roost." This composite shot depicts how Picasso's "Bust of a Woman" would have towered above the Fine Arts Building at USF. Photograph from the author's collection*

While Evangelist Billy Graham was in Tampa for a crusade in 1979, the Tampa Historical Society dedicated a historical marker on the site where he began his worldwide ministry by preaching to winos and derelicts on the street. The marker is erected at the present State Office Building at Franklin and Fortune streets, which is where the notorious Saratoga Bar was situated when Graham was getting his start while a student at Florida Bible Institute at Temple Terrace. This photo shows Dr. W. T. Watson (back to camera) leading the dedicatory prayer and (left to right) Florida Governor Bob Graham; Tampa Mayor William F. Poe; Mrs. Ruth Graham, wife of the evangelist; Billy Graham; and Hampton Dunn, who served as master of ceremonies. Photograph by Dan Fager, the Tampa Tribune

When Bob Martinez was a pupil at Tampa Bay Boulevard Grade School, he served on the school safety patrol. And in September 1980, after he had been Mayor of Tampa for some time, he revisited his old school, once again donned the uniform of a safety patrol, and assisted his nephew, Jimmy Vining, now a pupil and patrol at the school, in raising the flag on opening day. Martinez presently is a Republican candidate for Governor of Florida. Photograph by Skip Gandy, from the author's collection

A 1938 postcard shows the Bay View Hotel on Jackson Street when it was a popular hostelry and sported an electrified American flag on its roof at nighttime. The Bay View was built in 1912 and was originally going to be a liquor warehouse. Postcard from the author's collection

This photograph (copyright 1980 by Hampton Dunn) catches the instant the old Bay View Hotel started its collapse under the powerful implosion that meant sudden death for the landmark. Moments later, it was but a pile of rubble. It was razed to make way for the new skyscrapers that changed Tampa's skyline in the early 1980s. Photograph by the author

The Tampa Times

SATURDAY AUGUST 14, 1982 — FOUNDED 1893 — 90TH YEAR–NO. 162 — 15 CENTS

FINAL EDITION

So long and 30 from Times

By BOB TURNER
Staff Writer

Newspapers serve up a daily slice of life, and some of them — just like people and neighborhoods — flourish, grow old and die.

Newspapers go through good times and bad, good years and lean, but through all of it, the mission remains the same: Get the news and print it.

At one end of The Tampa Times news room, 21 pictures on the wall say well what this business is all about.

If you look there, you can see a welder and a tugboat at work, a halfback breaking into the secondary, a portrait of a wino down to his last cigarette and wishing he had another pint of booze, a little apprehensive about things.

And you can see a muscular construction worker topping out a building, a daintily clad ballet dancer, a boy pitching hay in a dairy barn and a murderer on death row gazing out a window and reflecting on what's left of his life.

One of those marvelous pictures is of a poor dumb ape, sitting all alone and holding his head in his massive, hairy paws, staring down into infinity with 5 million years of sadness on his furrowed, uncomprehending brow.

His mate is dead. He has lost his mate and he doesn't know what to do about it and there is nothing he can do about it.

To me, it is an incomparably great and moving photograph.

Felt like that

I think all of us here on The Times felt like that when we lost our paper the other day.

It hurt then and it still hurts. Bad.

Bruce Witwer, our managing editor and my veteran news colleague, said, "It's the worst day of my life. It was indescribably traumatic. You're dealing with people's lives and hearts, and a lot of people have worked their hearts out for this paper."

There's nothing we can do about it now either, although we know basically why it happened.

Witwer describes it succinctly:

• The Times has long had identification problems compared with The Tribune, "like a black cloud we were unable to shake."

• Television hurt. Marketing of The Times wasn't successful.

• Toward the end, a deadline of 7:30 a.m. limited the amount of fresh news in the early edition of The Times, and some readers, particularly in the suburbs, regarded it as a rehash of what they already had seen in The Tribune.

Constant squeeze

The Times' hallmark has always been local news, and tightened home-edition deadlines kept a constant squeeze on the amount of late-morning and early-afternoon developments we could handle.

• Delivery problems and periodic price increases also hurt.

Witwer said that some years ago, editors made a major effort to radically change the design of the newspaper — probably to a tabloid — but for reasons unknown to him, it was never fully pursued.

Newspaper people have strong stomachs, strong opinions and strong hearts, and so even with more than enough anguish to go around and even with their notoriously fragile egos, Times staffers were up to the task of getting the paper out to the

See SO LONG, page 4A

Laid-off employees now 'just statistics'

By SUSAN SHULINS
Staff Writer

For a little more than three years, I was somebody doing something significant.

I had identity writing some of the stories that let people know more about their community.

Today I'll just be a statistic among the ranks of millions of unemployed Americans.

This is my last assignment for The Tampa Times — to write about how it feels to be laid off. About 60 of my fellow Tribune Co. employees also were told this week that they were terminated because The Times will cease publication. Many were Times and Tribune news reporters.

It hurts. It hurts to know another afternoon newspaper will be no longer. And it's scary — scary to know you have to look for another job.

"You lose your identity — you almost become a nobody," said Henry Howard, a reporter for the East Hillsborough Tribune for the last two years, now departing. "I enjoyed being a Tribune reporter. It lent itself to a certain amount of prestige."

Tom Jackson, Times executive sports editor, has had an "official tie" with The Times for 12 years. Before that he began delivering it on his bike as a teen-ager. Jackson, who has held his post for two years, is among the 18 Times editorial staffers to lose their jobs. "I feel like I lost a really good friend," he said of the paper's demise.

"My brother and I fought over The Times every afternoon," he remembered.

Most of the employees found out about their terminations and the paper's demise through staff meetings Wednesday with publisher Richard F. Pittman. For months gossip circulated that The Times would merge with the morning paper, The Tampa Tribune. But many of us scoffed at them as nothing but rumors.

"There were so many of them, you learned to ignore them," said Marcia Ford, a Times staffer since 1978.

We all wondered, though, if The Times would follow the fate of other afternoon newspapers.

"I thought it only happened to other newspapers. We were so competent," said Ford, who formerly was the chief of The Times' Lakeland bureau, closed earlier this year. Her last assignment was special projects reporter in Brandon.

See STATISTICS, page 13A

Fred Fox/TAMPA TIMES

Final conference

State Editor Joe Guidry, left, City Editor Al Christopher and layout editor Kim Wilson confer early this morning as to the content of today's final edition of The Times.

Proper timing graced the paper

By RICHARD BOCKMAN
Staff Writer

New Times Dollarwords Puzzle Appears on Page 2
The Tampa Times
President Kennedy Killed
Shot to Death by Hidden Assassin
U.S. Reds Swap Protests
THE TAMPA TIMES
Makes 3 Orbits, Lands Safely
Globe-Girdling U.S. Astronaut Capsule Plucked From Atlantic
Confident, Calm During Flight Prelude
IT'S SNOWING!
The Tampa Times
Snow stuns Tampans

President Nixon cooperated. So did Vice President Agnew. They knew how late The Times could hold final edition, and each resigned just in time.

The Iranians stretched things to the bitter end, but finally capitulated to the telepathy beamed across the Atlantic by Florida afternoon newspapers. The hostages cleared Iranian air space in time for the p.m.'s to trumpet the news.

Where The Tribune reports news around the clock, The Times is limited to about eight hours of reporting, from the middle of the night until about noon. Deadlines cannot be pushed too far or the paper doesn't reach front yards until after the television evening news.

Tragedy by day across the Atlantic means tragedy reported in Florida afternoon newspapers, while the morning papers sit tight for 24 hours. Tampa awoke to the death of Anwar Sadat Oct. 6. He was shot at midday in Egypt, or 6:40 a.m. in Tampa. Even then The Times led with the cautious headline, "Sadat reported dead," because of conflicting reports of his status.

Pope John Paul II was shot at 5:30 p.m. in Italy, shortly before noon here, giving The Times about an hour to get together a story under the headline, "Pope shot twice in side at Vatican; suspect held."

From disaster to triumph, proper timing has graced The Times.

"30 known dead as freighter hits Skyway, span collapses."

"Snow stuns Tampans," the freaky Florida morning of Jan. 17, 1977.

"Fired police vice man murdered at his home," the killing of Richard Cloud.

"Glenn Makes 3 Orbits, Lands Safely," the space agency honoring The Times' polite request for a morning liftoff.

Former circulation director Vic Leavengood remembers scanning the wire services at lunchtime, in The Times newsroom after the paper had already been put to bed Nov. 22, 1963. The wires carried an alarm: President Kennedy had been shot.

Leavengood, now treasurer for General Telephone Co. of Florida, remembers his assistant, Tom Sherrill, immediately calling in the street sale supervisors to plan distribution of an extra edition.

Sherrill grabbed the first batch of 30-odd papers that rolled off the presses, with Leavengood right behind with the next batch.

See TIMING, page 13A

Carrier to continue hitting the bricks

By DAVID DAHL
Staff Writer

Harry Siders, newspaper carrier, will don the banner of a different publication Monday after 24 years of hawking The Tampa Times from his green and yellow sack.

Siders — he of the trademark safari hat and plodding gait — will wear the orange of The Tampa Tribune Monday, continuing his tradition as the only carrier for the company who makes his way by foot.

The other carriers use cars and trucks to distribute the 23,800 or so copies of The Times and 186,000-plus copies of the Tribune.

The 59-year-old Siders eschews that style. No look-alike convenience stores or front-yard tosses on his route.

His is a more elite clientele: the employees and shopgoers who make downtown Tampa their turf during the daylight hours.

Twice a day he makes his rendezvous in the underbelly of the Tribune building to pick up the two editions of The Times and then carry them on to downtown offices and a street corner.

On Thursday, the day after the news about The Times' demise circulated among the circulators, Siders honored a reporter's request to accompany him on his route to distribute the second edition of the paper.

The papers came off the presses and down the hatch at 12:58. Within minutes, Siders was afoot, with 50 copies in his ink-stained sack.

He shifted into low gear as he stepped up the Parker Street grade and onto Kennedy Boulevard. He told one interested passer-by that his job was OK, then spat on the sidewalk and continued on, his face already reddened by the 87-degree heat.

The heat didn't stop him, though. You can't dally in a job like Siders'.

"I can't walk as fast as I used to," Siders said, though he's still proud of the miles he logs in his black and white gym shoes.

Siders knows the penalty for not hustling. One fellow carrier was "retired" a few years back for stopping to talk too much with people on the route.

See CARRIER, page 13A

Inside The Times

Business	Sec. D		
Editorials	6,7A		
Latin Page	12A		
Classifieds	2D	Movies	5B
Comics	10A,11B	Quest	Sec. B
Deaths	13A	Television	4B

Poor circulation spelled the death of Tampa's afternoon newspaper, the Tampa Times, *after ninety years of impressive service to the city and state. The final edition served as its own obituary on Saturday, August 14, 1982. The* Tampa Times *front page, from the author's collection*

Meet George M. Steinbrenner III, Tampa resident and owner of the New York Yankees. The colorful sportsman and businessman also purchased Tampa Bay Downs racetrack and the Bay Harbor Inn and is chairman of the board of American Shipbuilding Co. He also contributes to the city's cultural and social life. Photograph from the author's collection

A delightful bundle of beauty and brains is Tampa's gorgeous Lisa Valdez—the "Miss Florida" reigning in early 1985. Twenty-two years old and the daughter of Mr. and Mrs. Rudy Valdez, Lisa previously held the titles of "Miss Florida State University," "Miss Tallahassee," and "Miss Manatee County." She was a high honors student both at Chamberlain High School in Tampa and at FSU. She is a devout member of the Spencer Memorial Baptist Church. Her winning talent is popular singing. She plans to earn a master's degree in public relations and sales promotion. Photograph from the author's collection

This early post card shows a bird's-eye view of Tampa, looking east from Tampa Bay Hotel. From the author's collection

Tampa's downtown skyline looked like this nearly 100 years ago. This view looks east from the Tampa Bay Hotel. The Hillsborough River is in the foreground and the Lafayette Street Bridge (now Kennedy Boulevard) is seen at right. The Sacred Heart Catholic Church is in the far background, center. Photograph from the author's collection

A new skyline was emerging in downtown Tampa in 1983 when this scene was photographed. This is a view from a building west of the University of Tampa, looking east. The university, formerly the Tampa Bay Hotel, is seen in the foreground. Skyscrapers of glass and steel puncture the skyline as the city goes through a metamorphosis. Photograph courtesy of Bill Stoeltzing, Bryn-Alan Studios, from the author's collection

Moonlight on Tampa Bay makes a memorable scene for visitors along Tampa's Bayshore Boulevard. This photograph was taken in the 1950s by Emmett Mattes, photographer for the Tampa Daily Times, *but the scene continues to be repeated any moonlit night nowadays. Photograph by Emmett Mattes, the* Tampa Daily Times, *from the author's collection*

Bibliography

The Associated Press Sports Staff. *A Century of Sports*. New York: The Plimpton Press, 1971.

Bachman, Harold B. *The Biggest B-O-O-M in Dixie*. Jacksonville: Paramount Press, 1968.

Brinton, Daniel G. *A Guide-Book of Florida and the South for Tourists, Invalids and Emigrants*. Bicentennial Floridiana Facsimile Series. Gainesville: The University Presses of Florida, 1978.

Brown, Charles H. *The Correspondent's War*. New York: Charles Scribner's Sons, 1967.

Brown, Warren J. *Florida's Aviation History, The First One Hundred Years*. Largo, FL: Aero-Medical Consultants, Inc., 1980.

Church, George B., Jr. *The Life of Henry Laurens Mitchell, Florida's 16th Governor*. New York: Vantage Press, Inc., 1978.

Cooper, Russell M., and Fisher, Margaret B. *The Vision of a Contemporary University*. Tampa: University Presses of Florida, 1982.

Covington, James W., and Laub, C. Herbert. *The Story of the University of Tampa*. Tampa: The University of Tampa Press, 1955.

Covington, James W. *The Story of Southwestern Florida, Vol. I*. New York: Lewis Historical Publishing Co., Inc., 1957.

Under the Minarets. Tampa: The University of Tampa, 1981.

Del Rio, Emilio. *Yo Fui Uno De Los Fundadores De Ybor City:* Tampa: 1972.

Dunn, Hampton. *WDAE—Florida's Pioneer Radio Station*. Tampa: Fort Brooke Press, Rounsaville Radio, Inc., 1972.

Yesterday's Tampa. Miami: E. A. Seemann Publishing, Inc., 1972.

Yesterday's St. Petersburg: Miami: E. A. Seemann Publishing, Inc., 1973.

Yesterday's Clearwater. Miami: E. A. Seemann Publishing, Inc., 1973.

Wish You Were Here—A Grand Tour of Early Florida Via Old Postcards. St. Petersburg: Byron Kennedy & Company, 1981.

Gray, Lt. Edgar. *The Tampa Fire Fighters*. Tampa: Paleveda Printing Co., 1972.

Grismer, Karl H. *The Story of St. Petersburg*. St. Petersburg: P. K. Smith & Co., 1948.

Tampa, *A History of the City of Tampa and the Tampa Bay Region*. St. Petersburg: The St. Petersburg Printing Co., 1950.

Hillsborough County Planning Commission. *Hillsborough County's Historic Heritage*. Tampa: Hillsborough County Planning Commission, 1974.

Junior League of Tampa, Inc. *Tampa, a Town on Its Way*. Tampa: Hillsboro Printing Co., 1971.

Kaese, Harold. *Famous American Athletes of Today, Sixth Series*. Boston: L. C. Page & Company, 1938.

Lanier, Sidney. *Florida, Its Scenery, Climate and History, 1875*, Bicentennial Floridiana Facsimile Series. Gainesville: University of Florida Press, 1973.

Poems of Sidney Lanier. Edited by his wife. New York: Charles Scribner's Sons, 1903.

Lowry, Sumter L. *Ole 93*. Tampa: Privately published, 1970.

McKay, D. B. *South Florida, Its Builders, Its Resources, Its Industries and Climatic Advantages*. Tampa: *The Tampa Daily Times*, 1924.

McKay, D. B. *Pioneer Florida*. Tampa: The Southern Publishing Co., 1959.

Moore, Colleen. *Silent Star Colleen Moore*. New York: Doubleday & Company, Inc., 1968.

Morris, Allen. *Florida Handbook, Seventh Edition, 1979-80*. Tallahassee: The Peninsular Publishing Co., 1979.

Muniz, Jose Rivero. *The Ybor City Story*. Translated by Fernandez, Eustasio, and Beltran, Henry. Tampa: Privately Printed, 1976.

Newton, V. M., Jr. *Crusade for Democracy*. Ames, Iowa: The Iowa State University Press, 1961.

Pizzo, Tony. *Tampa Town 1824-1886, The Cracker Village With a Latin Accent*. Miami: Hurricane House Publishers, Inc., 1968.

Powell, Evanell Klintworth. *Tampa That Was. . .History and Chronology Through 1946*. Boynton Beach, FL: Star Publishing Co., Inc., 1973.

Reese, M. Lisle. *Bean Soup or Florida With a Spanish Accent*. Jacksonville: Crawford Publishing Company, 1964.

Robinson, Ernest L. *History of Hillsborough County, Florida*. St. Augustine: The Record Co., 1928.

Skelton, Betty. *Little Stinker*. Winter Haven, FL: Cross Press, 1977.

Spaulding, Dr. Frederic H. *A University is Born. The University of Tampa from Inception to Adolescence*. Tampa: Privately Printed, 1974.

Tampa Historical Society. *Sunland Tribune*. Tampa: Joe B. Klay and Sons, 1977, 1978, 1979, 1980, 1981.

Tebeau, Charlton W. *Florida's Last Frontier, The History of Collier County*. Miami: The University of Miami Press, 1957.

Turner, Nancy. *The History of Ye Mystic Krewe of Gasparilla, 1904-1979*. Tampa: The Cider Press, Inc., 1979.

Verrill, A. Hyatt. *Romantic and Historic Florida*. New York: Dodd, Mead & Company, 1935.

Warren, Fuller. *How to Win in Politics*. Tallahassee: The Peninsular Publishing Co., 1949.

Zaharias, Babe Didrikson. *This Life I've Led, My Autobiography*. As Told to Harry Paxton, New York: A. S. Barnes and Company, 1955.

Index

A
Abbott, William B., Jr., 127
Allen, Dr. and Mrs. John S., 199, 202, 208
Alvarez, Judy, 203
American Legion, 70, 172
American Red Cross, 39, 156, 204
Anti Evolution Bill,, 85
Arnade, Dr. Charles, 12
Ashley, William, 20
Askew, Gov. Reubin, 206
Atlantic Coast Line Railroad, 86, 87

B
Bachman, Col. Harold B., 90
Baker, George T. (Ted), 110
Ballast Point Pier, 72
Bananas, 115
Bank of Tampa, 192
Barbershop Quartet, 165
Barcelona Spanish Restaurant, 186
Barton, Clara, 39
Baseball, 32, 75, 174
Batista, Fulgencio, 137, 194
Bayshore Baptist Church, 92
Bayshore Boulevard, 96, 99
Bay View Hotel, 68, 119, 216
B & B Super Market, 192
Beachey, Lincoln, 59
Bellamy, Francis, 103
Beaulah Baptist Institutional Church, 153
Bickel, Karl A., 135
Biglow Mansion, 78
Biglow, Silas L., 78
Big Orange, 114
Billy Bowlegs, 15
Blakeslee, Carl W., 136
Blandy, Richard, 97
Boggs, Otis, 188
Bonfoey and Elliott, 60
Bourquardez, Constant and Laurel, 47
Bourquardez, Phil R., 156
Branch, Sen. John, 187
Branch Opera House, 21, 29, 48
Brandon, Jim, 21
Brewster Vocational School, 154, 209
Brooke, Col. George M., 11, 15
Brooke, Col. George M., Jr., 16
Brorein, Carl D., 136, 160
Brorein, W.G., 45, 96, 113
Briwn, C. A. "Smitty," 107
Brulett, Mrs. Phyllis, 185
Bucholtz, Fritz, 56
Burnett, Jean, 168
Busch Gardens, 205
Bustillo Brothers and Diaz Cigar Factory, 58

C
Caballeros de la Luz, 165
Carlton, Doyle E., Jr., 137, 200
Carlton, Gov. Doyle E., 97, 137, 200, 206, 214
Carnes, Captain, 62
Carnes, Queen Mary, 49, 50
Carrollwood, 202, 204
Carter, Gen. Jesse, 17
Carty, Kate (Mrs. T. V. R.), 45
Celi, Don Francisco Maria, 12
Centro Asturiano, 70, 154
Chamberlin, Col. Clarence, 123
Chamber of Commerce, 153, 173, 175
Chancey, Mayor R. E. L., 102, 111, 123, 141, 145, 156
Chavez, Helen, 64
Chitwood, Joie, Sr., 171, 172
Christmas, 176, 177, 202
Cigar Industry, 58, 62, 70
Citizens Bank & Trust Co., 69, 91
Cincinnati Reds, 75, 163
Citrus, 88
Citrus Park School, 209
Civilian Conservation Corps, 111
City Hall, 48, 60, 75
Clendenin, James A., 6, 7, 9
Cline, Carolyn, 215
Cold, Jean Marie "Sammye," 200
Colescott, Dr. James A., 124
Coller, Levi and Nancy Dixon, 18
Collins, Gov. LeRoy, 197
Colonial Hotel, 59
Colonnade, The, 199
Columbia Restaurant, 131, 203
Company "H," 65
Cone, Gov. Fred, P., 112, 136
Cone, J. L., 62
Coulson, Dean John, 105
Court House, Hillsborough County, 33, 60, 75, 130, 173, 186
Craft's Hotel, 21
Crystal Ball Restaurant, 60, 130
Cuban Club, 123, 166
Culverhouse, Hugh, 212
Curtis, G. Dave, 153

D
Daniels, Oscar, Drydock Co., 63
Dantzler, Ray, 188
Daughters of the American Revolution, 17, 180
Davis, Capt. Ben T., 109
Davis, Lt. Gen. Benjamin O., Jr., 208
Davis Causeway, 99, 109
Davis, D. P., 69, 77, 83
Davis Islands, 77, 82, 83, 116, 152
Davis, Richard Harding, 43
Davis, Sam, 145
Dean, Miss Annie Laurie, 39, 41
Delta Kappa, 161
Dempsey, Jack, 122, 181
DeSoto Hotel, 157
Dies, U.S. Rep. Martin, 138
Dixie Tennis Tournament, 116
Dodd Motor Company, 79
Dolcater, John, 173
Dreves, Fred, 76
Drew Field, 74, 93, 135, 148, 149, 153, 163
Dunn, Hampton, 7, 12, 187, 204, 215, 216, 225
Duval, Jewelry Co., 144

E
Eastern Air Lines, 128, 145, 182, 209
Egypt Temple Shrine, 181, 187
Ekdahl, Margaret (Mickey), 99, 102
Elections, 111, 156, 173, 207
Elks Lodge, 60, 75, 130, 162
Emery, Simmons & Emery Store, 21
Emmanuel, Michel, 99
End, George K., 132
Exchange National Bank, 32

F
Falk, O., 44, 150
Falor's Triple XXX Root Beer, 103
Farnell, J. Crockett, 155
Farrior, J. Rex, 151
Fellows, Bob, 13
Figueredo, Lou, 101, 157
Fire Department, Tampa, 48, 52, 76
First Baptist Church, 23, 87, 112, 118
First National Bank, 48, 64, 69
Flagpole Sitter, 97
Fleischman, Sol, 95, 141, 145, 164, 181, 188, 195, 203
Florida Bible Institute, 133, 215
Florida State Fair, 45, 75, 79, 113, 122, 136, 139, 169, 172, 183, 193, 204, 209, 214
Florida Theatre, 151
Florida Trebles, 165
Ford, Al, 208
Ford, Eddie, 105
Ford, U.S. Vice President Gerald, 210
Ford's, Larry, 119
Forest Hills Golf and Country Club, 171
Fort Brooke, 11, 16
Fort Dade, 37
Fort Foster, 17
Fort Homer Hesterly Armory, 189, 193, 196
Foulkes, The Rev. John, S.J., 45
Fowler, Cody, 199
Franco, Jose S., 84
Franklin Theatre, 90
Frierson, Mrs. J. Roy, 180
Frost, M. M. (Jack), 145

G
Gaither, King W. C., 49
Gandy Bridge, 69, 77
Gannon, Francis J., 160
Garcia, Manuel, 167
Garlits, Big Daddy Don, 213
Gasoline, 142
Gasparilla, 49, 113, 178, 180, 183, 189, 192
Gasparilla Motorcycle Club, 140
Gibbons, Sam M., 187, 202, 206
Golden Hills, 82
Gomez, Tommy, 147
Gonzmart, Cesar and Adela, 131, 203
Goody Goody, 104
Gordon Keller School of Nursing, 144
Graham, Evangelist Billy, 133, 215, back end paper
Graham, Gov. Bob, 215
Grange, "Red," 81
Grant, Bitsy, 116
Grasso, Frank, 132, 165
Gray, Don, 13
Gray, Lt. Edgar, 52
Gray, Robert (Bo), 207
Greco, Mayor Dick, 196, 208
Green, Truman, 160

Griffith, Kathleen, 209
Gulf Life Insurance Co., 76

H
Hagerman, Will Kay, 146
Hale Drug Co., 100
Hale, Dean Morris S., 114
Hall, Jon, 120, 132
Happy's Corner, 158
Harrison, John N., 145, 152
Harrison, Samuel G., 175
Hatcher, Mary, 165
Hatton, L. M., Jr., 92
Hatton, L. M., Sr., 92
Hatton, Rondo, 65, 97
HavaTampa Cigar Co., 137, 200
"Hell Harbor," 97
Helms, Dr. John S., 78
Henderson Air Field, 198
Hernandez, Casimiro, Jr., 131
Hesterly, Col. Homer W., 94, 193
Hiers, Sheriff L. M., 94
Higgins, Coach Nash, 116, 163
Hi Hat Club, 157
Hillsborough High School, 56, 57, 105, 155
Hillsborough River, 22
Hixon, Mayor Curtis, 156, 163, 169, 170, 183
Holsum Bakers, 176, 177
Home Guard, 145, 152
Honeymoon Isle, 166
Holland, U. S. Sen. Spessard, 200
Hood, Mrs. Bertha F., 174
Hotel Le Fort, 24
Hurricanes, 69, 70

I
Italian Club, 76

J
Jackson, Frank D., 39, 55, 62, 190
Jackson, John, 19, 20
Jackson, Kate, 45
Jackson, Richard D. (Dick), 66, 165, 205
Jago, Coach Gordon, 211
Jail, Hillsborough County, 94
James, Mr. and Mrs. Frederick J., 51, 77, 94
Jannus, Tony, 43, 63
Johns, Sen. Charley E., 203
Johns Committee, 203
Johnson, Rep. Tom J., Jr., 187
Jones, Police Chief J. C. (Jimmie), 33

K
Kaiser Automobile, 169
Kefauver Crime Investigating Committee, 151, 179, 180
Keller, Gordon, 53, 54
Keller, Sara Lykes (Hobbs), 77
Kennedy, President John F., 206
Key Club, 85
King, Henry, 97
Klintworth, Mrs. C. Verne, 79
Knight, Col. Peter O., 34, 76, 128
Kruse, Henry, 42, 43, 111
Ku Klux Klan, 124

L
Lafayette Street Bridge, 26, 36, 87, 218
Lambright, Ed D., 117
Langford, Frances, 121, 132
Lanier, Sidney, 20
Las Novedadas, 167
Latin American Fiesta, 137, 189, 194
Leavine, Benjamin Franklin, 94
Licata, Philip F., 76
Lighthouse, Egmont Key, 44
Lincoln Theatre, 160
Lindbergh, Col. Charles A., 88
"Little Stinker," 170
Lopez, Al, 195
Lord, Bobby, 193
Lowry, Patricia, 183
Lowry, Sumter L., Jr., 56, 65, 76, 94, 172, 197
Luttrall, Cowboy, 181
Lykes Brothers, 136, 200
Lykes, Dr. Howell Tyson, 24, 25, 136
Lykes, Joseph T., 200

Mc
McAteer, Capt. T. G., 231
McCarty, Gov. Dan, 173
McCurdy, Jack Douglas, 59
McDuffie, Ann, 104
McEwen, Tom, 138, 195
McGregor, Bonnie, 206
McKay, D. B., 76, 88, 96, 111
McKay, Ernest G., 144
McKay, Capt. James, 25
McKay, John, 212
McMullen, Norma, R.N., 156

M
Maas Brothers, 38, 96, 102, 150
Mabry, Capt. Dale, 74
MacDill Field, front end paper, 74, 99, 135, 138, 140, 141, 142, 146, 158, 170, 208
Mackey, Dr. Maurice Cecil, 208
Marbourg, Bill, 106
Marti, Jose, 35
Martin, J. R., and Co., 51
Martin, Gov. John W., 96
Martinez, Mayor Bob, 216
Mason, George H., 117
Mattes, Emmett, 219
Meadows, The Rev. S. G., 59
Meighen, Miss Isobel, 144
Memorial Highway, 70, 93
Merchants Association of Tampa, 192
Merrill, Herman, Family, 94
Middleton Senior High School, 197
Miller, R. W., 55
Mirabella, Queen Marie Joann, 194
"Miss America," 99, 102, 215
"Miss Florida," 102, 215, 217
"Miss Tampa," 72, 77, 102, 168, 200, 206, 215
Mitchell, Gov. Henry Laurens, 35, 174
Mitchell, Joe, 109
Mitchell, L. Spencer, 117
Mixson, T. G., 153
Mizell, Hubert, 213
Moncrief, Dr. Adiel J., 118
Moody, Rep. James S., 187
Moore, Colleen, 66, 67
Morrison's Cafeteria, 121
Murphree, Conrad, 118
Murray, J. A. "Jock," 127

N
Nance, Dr. E. C., 168
National Airlines, 99, 110, 163, 194
National Guard, 94, 111, 193
National Register of Historic Places, 60, 75, 78
Nebraska Hotel, 101
Neely, Gertrude, R.N., 156
Newberry, J. J., Store, 143
Newton, V. M. "Red," 138
Norton, Charles E. "Pete," 138
Nuccio, Mayor Nick C., 196
Nuccio, Vincent, 205

O
Oaklawn Cemetery, 35
Office, The, 119
Oldroyd, Evan Clark, 4
Olds, R. E., 81
Oldsmar, 81
Osceola, Joe Dan, 16
Our Lady of Mercy Church, 34
Owens, Dr. Bob, 210

P
Palma Ceia Golf and Country Club, 195
Palmetto Hotel, 24
Pan American Airways, 96, 99
Parslow, Paul I., 84
Pedroso, Pauline, 35
Peninsular Telephone Co., 113, 136
Petteway, Judge W. Raleigh, 112
Phillips Field, 190
Phillips, Queen Kathleen, 50
Phosphate, 108
Picasso, Pablo, 215
Piggly Wiggly, 132
Pioneer Tire Co., 97
Pizzo, Tony, 12, 16
Plant Field, 75, 163, 183
Plant, Henry B., 26, 28, 120
Plant High School, 120, 137, 170, 199, 200
Plant Park, 89, 90, 148, 175, 206
Plant System of Railway, Steamer & Steamship Lines, 27, 30, 31, 39
Plattner, Max, 117
Poe, Mayor William F., 215
Police Department, Tampa, 33, 48, 71, 100, 107, 187
Population, Tampa, 23
Port Tampa, 28, 108
Port Tampa Inn, 28, 29
Port Tampa Methodist Church, 191
Power, Tyrone, 168

R
Rand, Sally, 169
Rattlesnake, Florida, 132
Rawls, Dennis B., 120
Rawls, Katherine (Katy), 103
Red Mill, 101
Reed, B. Marion, Funeral Home, 94, 120
Reeves, Gilvie L., 183

Resnick's Restaurant, 173
Richardson, Josiah, 101, 202
Rickenbacker, Capt. Eddie V., 182
Ripley, Robert L., "Believe It Or Not!," 97, 101
Rockport, 108
Rondanzo, Santo, 13
Roosevelt, Teddy, 167
Rotary Club of Tampa, 70, 93, 113, 173
Rough Riders, 167
Rowlett, Dr. William M., 144
Royal American Shows, 169
Rubin, Jose, 122
Rubin, Manuel, 120, 122, 137
Rubin's Spanish Restaurant, 121, 122
Ruth, Babe, 121

S
St. Joseph's Hospital, 188
St. Joseph's School, 168
St. Petersburg *Times,* 211, 213
Sacred Heart Catholic Church, 45, 218
Sanchez, Manuel, 139
Sanderson, Watts, 152
Sandler, Judge Harry N., 76
Scharri Zedek Synagogue, 157
Seale, J. Leland, 62
Seaplane Base, 96
Sedlmayr, Sr., Carl J., 169
Seminole Heights, 115
Seminole Sandwich Shop, 115
Seminole Theatre, 115, 158
Shafter, Gen. W. R., 36
Shipbuilding, 63, 127, 128, 160
Sholtz, Gov. Dave, 102, 114, 151
Sigma Kappa Nu, 139
Sigman, Dot, 139
Skelton, Betty, 166, 170
Skyline, Tampa, 87, 175, 218
Smiley, David E., 192
Snow, 214
Solomon, Freddie, 210
South Florida Fair, 59, 79, 80
Southern Songsters, 79
Spanish American War, 35, 36, 37, 38, 40
Spaulding, Dr. Frederic H., 105
Spencer Memorial Baptist Church, 217
Spicola, Tom, 174
Spoto, Dick, 155
Stalnaker, Leo, Sr., 17, 85
Stage Coaches, 19
Star Light Club, 143
Steamers, 23, 24, 53, 55, 68, 80
Steinbrenner, George M., III, 217
Stowers Funeral Home, 21
Stringer, Dr. Sheldon, 17
Stumpf, Miss Florence, 149
Sulphur Springs, 59, 71, 73, 101, 112, 133, 202
Sulphur Springs Baptist Church, 133
Sulphur Springs Hotel, 101
Sunset Beach, 72

T
Tampa Aero Club, 88
Tampa Automobile and Golf Club, 61
Tampa Airport Marriott Hotel, 207
Tampa Bay Buccaneers, 212, 213
Tampa Bay Downs, 81
Tampa Bay Hotel, 11, 26, 27, 29, 33, 39, 40, 56, 69, 89, 99, 105, 106, 125, 218
Tampa Bay Rowdies, 211
Tampa Beach, 81
Tampa Business College, 92, 142
The *Tampa Daily Times,* 50, 67, 76, 85, 95, 96, 97, 147, 164, 192, 197, 219
Tampa Electric Co., 34, 76, 103, 119, 120, 160, 164
Tampa Executives Club, 190
Tampa General Hospital, 78
Tampa Greyhound Track, 101, 110
Tampa Historical Society, 16, 34, 215
Tampa Housing Authority, 146
Tampa International Airport, 182, 207, 209
Tampa Municipal Auditorium, 96, 138, 149, 164
Tampa Municipal Hospital, 69, 78, 144
Tampa Silver Cornet Band, 29
Tampa Students Art Club, 50
Tampa Terrace Hotel, 87, 117, 147
Tampa Theatre, 91, 98, 99, 105
Tampa Tourist Center, 89, 148
Tampa *Times,* 204, 207, 214, 217
Tampa *Tribune,* 6, 7, 97, 104, 117, 118, 121, 126, 127, 132, 138, 147, 150, 160, 173, 182, 195, 203
Tampa Yacht and Country Club, 133
Tamiami Trail, 96
Temple Terrace, 82, 103, 133, 199, 215
Theodore Roosevelt School, 185
Thomas Jefferson Hotel, 184
Thompson, Woodrow, 147
Tinker, Gen. Clarence L., 138, 140, 141
Traynor, Frank M., 160

U
United Services Organization (USO), 159, 161, 163
University of Florida, 39, 90, 114, 116, 151, 188, 200, 207
University of South Florida, 179, 199, 202, 203, 208, 215
University of Tampa, 75, 99, 105, 106, 114, 125, 129, 138, 139, 161, 168, 170, 179, 206, 210, 218
USS Tampa, 43, 64, 172

V
Valdez, Lisa, 217
Vallina, Queen Hortense, 137
Vasta, The Rev. Achilles, 34
Velez, Lupe, 97
La Verbena del Tobaco, 139
Verne, Jules, 19
Victory National Life Insurance Co., 76
Victory Theatre, 95
V-J Day, 162

W
Walter, James W., 165
Wall, Dr. John P., 22, 60, 130
Wall, Mayor Perry G., 80, 88
Warner, Suzanne, 205
Warren, Gov. Fuller, 124, 173
Warren, James W., 183
Waterman, Jerome A., 96
Watson, Dr. W. T., 215
WDAE, 79, 90, 95, 117, 132, 141, 181, 187, 188, 192, 193, 195, 197, 208
WFLA, 109, 132
Wheeler, Gen. Joe, 36
White, George, 182
Whiteside, Dick, 199
Williams, Esther, 203
Wilson, Roland A., II, 66, 126
Wing, Mayor F. L., 54
Witt, Eli, 132
Wolf, Harold, 66
Wood, J. A., 33
Woolworth, F. W., 159
Works Progress Administration (WPA), 128, 193
World War I, 43, 64, 90
World War II, 74, 77, 109, 132, 135, 142, 145, 146, 147, 152, 153, 154, 156, 157, 158, 159, 160, 161, 163, 198
WRUF, 188
WSUN, 133, 208
WTVT-TV, 95, 181, 188

Y
Ybor City, 35, 52, 101, 162, 167
Ybor, V. Martinez, 34

Z
Zaharias, Babe and George, 171

Books by Hampton Dunn

Re-Discover Florida
WDAE—Florida's Pioneer Radio Station
Yesterday's Tampa
Yesterday's St. Petersburg
Yesterday's Clearwater
Florida Sketches
Yesterday's Tallahassee
Yesterday's Lakeland
Back Home—A History of Citrus County, Florida
Wish You Were Here—A Grand Tour of Early Florida Via Old Post Cards
Tampa—A Pictorial History

Educational Film Strip by Hampton Dunn

Florida—Treasureland in the Sun

About the Author

Hampton Dunn, a Florida native, has lived in Tampa for over fifty years; this fact in itself might be credential enough for an author to write a pictorial history of a town. But Dunn has even greater qualifications. Over a span of twenty-two years he acted as reporter, city editor, and managing editor of *The Tampa Daily Times,* a period which included four years as a major in the Air Force and a public relations officer in the Mediterranean theater. After leaving the newspaper in 1958, he was political commentator and news analyst for WCKT-TV in Miami. His line of work kept him at the scene of or aware of all newsworthy events and enabled him to rely on many photographs he himself has taken over the years. He has received an award from Associated Press and numerous other organizations. His collection of photos, which includes most of those of the Burgert Brothers and the Robertson and Fresh collections as well as his own, is thought to be one of the largest private collections of Florida historical photographs and is now in the Special Collections Department of the University of South Florida Library.

Dunn is now senior vice president and public relations director of the Peninsula Motor Club (AAA). He edits the club publication, *Florida Explorer,* and in the last fifteen years has written a dozen books and filmstrips about Florida's history and features. He holds office in numerous professional and civic organizations, such as the Historic Tampa/Hillsborough County Preservation Board, the Historic Pensacola Preservation Board, and the Historic Tallahassee Preservation Board. Honors have been bestowed upon him by many groups, to name a few—the American Association for State and Local History; the Florida, Tampa, Peace River Valley, and Polk County historical societies; and the United Daughters of the Confederacy. He was one of seventy-six designated as Florida Patriots by the Florida Bicentennial Commission and has received a Distinguished Public Service Award from the University of Tampa.

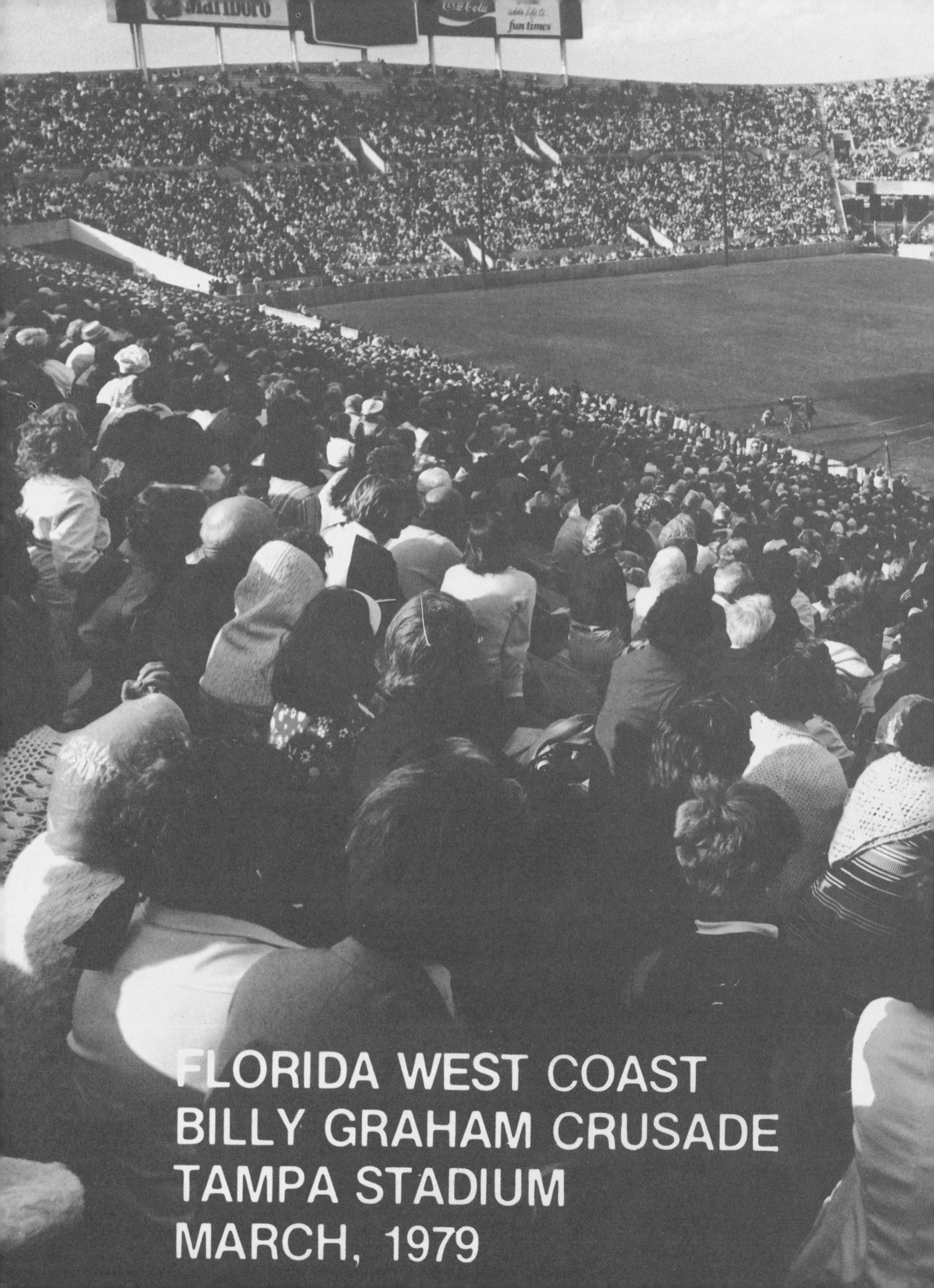

FLORIDA WEST COAST
BILLY GRAHAM CRUSADE
TAMPA STADIUM
MARCH, 1979